"An entertaining read, packed with interesting facts concerning Shakespeare's links with Oxford, the town and gown"

Paul Burge - BBC South today

"Following Shakespeare through Elizabethan and Jacobean Oxford, we discover delightful, informative and novel facets of the Bard's relationship with the great University town"

Simon Image - Shock Troupe theatre, Assistant Director

"As an Oxford man born and bred I found this to be a fantastic read. The Oxford Shakespeare knew, brimming with sex, scandal and religious upheaval"

Marty Emberton - Actor from The Kings Arms Players

Sweete Wittie Soules

Shakespeare's connections to Oxford, town, gown & shire.

Tom McDonnell

AUTOLYCUS BOOKS

2016

AUTOLYCUS BOOKS

First published 2016 by Autolycus Books

Copyright © 2016 Tom McDonnell

Cover image by Susannah Cartwright

Autolycus Books
28 Canning Crescent
Oxford OX14XB

The general editors of this book have been Adam Dale, Anna Soprano, Joseph Wilkins

Contents

Introduction

The richness of a country's culture is often measured by the success, dynamism and impact of its art. William Shakespeare's contribution to both England's culture and national identity is, on this basis, unsurpassed, and it is unsurprising that many different sections of English society claim him as their own. Modern day politicians quote his 'patriotic' speeches[1], while to many he is the poet of the people, born and raised in the Midlands, as English as Robin Hood, King Arthur and roast beef with mustard. Shakespeare is to some a conservative and to others a working class hero, with his humble beginnings and subsequent rise to prominence and wealth, despite the colossal gap between classes in Tudor England. Some, however, are uncomfortable with the notion that the national poet, the poster boy for English literature, is represented by a man who did not attend University. Some even make assertions that only an educated man could have written the works ascribed to Shakespeare.

Shakespeare's faith is also widely debated. Detail about his early life and family, as well as many references within his plays, suggest that Shakespeare was a secret Catholic. However, many refute this and argue that he was in fact a Protestant. Others even believe that he was an atheist. This book does not seek to resolve this frequently pondered question. What we should keep at the front of our minds is that religion was a huge part of early modern culture and so, regardless of his own beliefs, Shakespeare's life and works were deeply impacted by the events of the 16th and 17th centuries which saw the greatest cultural upheaval of the second millennium, the Reformation. It can therefore be said that Shakespeare did much of his writing in a 'Brave New World'[2] where religious institutions and traditions that had been preserved for centuries, were removed without a trace, in some cases overnight.

Shakespeare's innovative style and rich vocabulary reflects this changing cultural landscape. Though many of his story lines were patched together from old plays, borrowed from Greek classics, or, as with the majority of the history plays, inspired by the Holinshed Chronicles,[3] the rich tones of his language coupled with his natural aptitude for conveying a wide range of emotions added new depth to the characters he developed for the stage. Despite the talent of his contemporaries, none could match his gift for subtle nuance. Christopher Marlowe excelled with flowery high language and Ben Jonson's relentless wit trumped Shakespeare in the sardonic department, but the Stratford man brought a rich realism unrivalled by other writers of the time. One possible reason for this is that he was an actor before becoming a playwright. Whatever the explanation, his unique portrayal of the human condition has enthralled us for centuries. 'Shakespeare has no heroes; his scenes are occupied only by men'[4] stated the astute Samuel Johnson in the preface to his edition of Shakespeare's works. {1765}

As well as breaking the mould in terms of literature, Shakespeare's works also helped to shape and accelerate written English language, which was lingering in the shadows of Latin, still the first formal language. But despite all of this, Shakespeare was not particularly popular for many years after his death. Ben Jonson, Francis Beaumont and John Fletcher were the stars that shone at the time. A large portion of Shakespeare's plays would have been lost forever had it not been for two of Shakespeare's fellow actors and loyal friends, John Heminges and Henry Condell, who arranged the publication of his works in 1623, seven years after his death. Without the efforts of his old cronies, we might not have *Macbeth, The Tempest, Julius Caesar, Anthony and Cleopatra* or *Coriolanus*. The rumoured love child of Shakespeare, Oxford playwright William Davenant, also raised the Bard's profile in the mid-17th century before his popularity dwindled. It wasn't however, until the greatest Shakespearian actor of the 18th century, Samuel Johnson's close friend David Garrick, helped to cement the legendary reputation of Shakespeare, which continues to grow even today.

Garrick organised the first Shakespeare Jubilee in Stratford upon Avon to honour his hero in 1769. This seminal event massively popularised Shakespeare and started a snowball effect with similar festivals popping up all over the world, furthering Shakespeare's popularity.[5]

Ironically, Garrick lost a small fortune with the Stratford Jubilee, which was hampered by torrential rainfall. He did, however, recoup his losses and much more by staging a popular play about the Jubilee! Ben Jonson was certainly prophetic when he famously stated in the first folio preface that Shakespeare was 'a man not for an age but for all time'; since Garrick's festival, Shakespeare's fame has eclipsed the competition.

Though Shakespeare's status and legacy as a literary giant is undisputed, little is known about the ordinary man himself. Nicholas Rowe, Thomas Betterton, Richard Davies, Thomas Fuller, William Fulham and the two Oxford antiquaries Anthony A. Wood and John Aubrey are the earliest biographers who provided us with all manner of weird and wonderful legends about Shakespeare, from his penchant for deer poaching to his career as a school master in Lancashire. The infamously unreliable but highly amusing duo, Anthony A Wood and John Aubrey will crop up time and time again throughout this book.

Throughout the years, aspects of Shakespeare's life in Stratford upon Avon and London have been thoroughly covered, but there are not many references in print to his visits to Oxford or how some rumoured events that took place in the city of dreaming spires may have possibly shaped his life and works. As the curator of the medieval Carfax tower, which stands in Oxford's city centre, I have been asked all manner of questions from a wide range of visiting tourists, eager to climb the ninety-nine steps to catch a bird's eye view of the city. Most tourists ask to be directed to Christ Church college with its grand dining hall, now famed as a Harry Potter film location. Many ask for the location of the University, unaware that Oxford University surrounds them at all sides and comprises thirty-eight separate colleges, alongside University museums, libraries and faculty buildings. Very occasionally I have been asked for directions to the painted room in which Shakespeare resided on his visits to Oxford. This question initially caught me out and it was to my surprise that others involved in tourism in Oxford knew little of Shakespeare's visits. So I decided to undertake some research to find out more about Shakespeare's seemingly mysterious connection with Oxford, and to my great delight I have been astounded by the stories I have discovered. This book is my compartmentalization of the stories that connect Shakespeare with the town, the gown and the shire. I believe this is the first time a book has been written covering this subject as its main focus and I hope the readers will find the finished product half as entertaining as I have found the process of compiling over the last six years.

It is no surprise that Oxford, with its boast of many famous and wealthy alumni over the centuries, has attained some very rare and precious treasures, including some relevant to Shakespeare's life and times. What are thought to be the first biographical writings on Shakespeare lay under lock and key at Oriel college and extremely rare architectural designs of the Blackfriars theatre have been discovered in Worcester College library, which have changed the way we thought Jacobean theatres would have looked, as well as providing the master builder Peter McCurdy with a blueprint for the Globe's sister theatre – The Sam Wanamaker Playhouse theatre. The first acknowledged painting of an actor (Henry Harris) in Shakespearean costume resides in the president's office in Magdalen College. A battered first folio sits in the Bodleian library, as does a rare copperplate which inspired Gregory Doran's reworking of Shakespeare's lost play *Cardenio*.[6] The University also brings forth an abundance of fascinating stories involving Shakespeare, from his connections to Jesuits determined to overthrow Queen Elizabeth to his rumoured involvement in writing sections of the King James authorised bible.

It is not solely the University that provides us with insightful tales; the town itself also offers much intrigue. First of all, the aforementioned mysterious painted room, which Shakespeare is said to have slept in on his journeys from London to Stratford, largely untouched since Elizabethan times. There is also the original font of St Martin's church (now in St Michael at the North Gate, in central Oxford), in which Shakespeare would have witnessed the baptism of his godson, or love child if the rumours are to be believed. The King's Arms pub is also known for having played host to a very special performance of *Hamlet*; the world's premier performance outside of the capital.

If we look beyond the city walls we can also dig up marvellous anecdotes from the Shire: a hilarious confrontation between Shakespeare and the local constables of England's 'dirtiest town;' Grendon Underwood, a brutal fight in Thame which ended in tragedy but may have kickstarted Shakespeare's acting career in the theatre; and a play entitled *The Two Angry Women of Abingdon* written by an Oxford playwright, which may have provided Shakespeare with some much needed inspiration when the need to please Queen Elizabeth came with a deadline. All this and so much more will be covered within the following pages.

1. Oxford In Shakespeare's Time

Oxford in Shakespeare's time would have been vastly different to the tourist filled hustle bustle of a crowded small city, which now boasts 28,000 students. The entire population in Tudor Oxford was around 3,400, regarded then as a rather large town. A significant number of medieval college buildings were demolished and replaced in the 18th and 19th centuries, and Victorian architects in particular have a lot to answer for when it comes to short-sighted planning and the destruction of buildings that many believe should have been preserved. Oxford's town planners have constructed many monstrosities over the last century; garish shopping centres and multi-storey car parks that have little in keeping with the rest of the city's ornate architecture. But how beautiful was Oxford in the 16th century?

Oxford, like the rest of England, would have been a very noisome place indeed, though not quite as pungent as London, which a city traveller could smell before he could see it. Horse excrement would have been splattered all over the extremely muddy grounds, with the terrible stench intensified by over-ground sewage. The centre of Oxford has a hilltop effect due to sixteen different levels of earth having been layered between Saxon times and Elizabethan days, which was created for sewage to slide down into the city outskirts. The ground was also raised to prevent the city from flooding, a common occurrence these days, though Oxford's boggy lands have been infamous since the Roman invaders, who didn't stick around too long, finding the land undesirable and difficult to build upon. It is clear to see that Oxford's roads have a Saxon origin as opposed to Roman; the roads around the city are winding as opposed to straight.

To the North of the city, Broad Street was host to horse fairs and, until the creation of the covered market in the late 1800s, cattle and pigs were openly slaughtered on the site of what was the old city ditch. To the South of St. Aldates, which was at the time called Fish Street, as it hosted the fish market, was the Guildhall, where the town hall sits today. A five-minute walk to the west of St. Aldates leads to the Oxford castle ruins and former prison site where medical students would have waited feverishly around the gallows of the castle mound, ready to snatch the body of a convict to practise their medical experiments, sometimes pulling impatiently on the feet of the hanging felon. There were also many taverns and churches throughout the city, with the city wall, which divided the city and University, exemplifying the divide between the members of the University and townsfolk.

Crime was rife among the streets and prostitutes would have walked up and down what is now Magpie Lane, off the High Street, perhaps purposefully positioned to tempt the unmarried members of the University. Oxford's oldest wooden structure on 26–27 Cornmarket street (now a sandwich shop) was the notorious New Inn, the top floor of which was infamous for housing a popular brothel. Armed thieves and highway men would have prowled the North Gate of the city, exactly where the Royal Oak public house now sits, waiting to attack and relieve unsuspecting travellers of their belongings. Though tensions had eased somewhat between the town and gown since the University's twelfth century foundations, violence between the two parties was not uncommon, with tensions exacerbated by the fact that University members were governed by church law as opposed to state law. This was a source of constant irritation for the locals who felt that the students could get away with murder, literally. In addition, the average strength of beer was around 11 per cent and was drunk copiously due to the foulness of the water[7], which probably didn't help matters. Nevertheless, many of the townsfolk were craftsmen and therefore largely dependent on the University for their livelihood.

The University would have been much smaller in Shakespeare's time, with seventeen colleges established by 1610. Today, Oxford's Radcliffe Square is one of the most beautiful collections of buildings in Europe; its postcard picture highlights include James Gibbs' delightful dome-shaped library, the Radcliffe Camera. However, where beautiful All Souls college sits, with its Christopher Wren sundial adorning the vast quad, and Oxford's version of the Bridge of Sighs connects two parts of Hertford college, Shakespeare would have seen a shoddy scattering of small wooden houses resembling a shanty town.

Carfax tower, Oxford

The students were also a great deal younger than today's scholars; most students started when they were about twelve years old, fresh from grammar school, and the degrees would have taken around a decade to complete. The exams would have been oral as opposed to scribed and the amount of information that had to be retained was vast by today's standards, Curfew for the students was strictly 9pm and anyone caught returning late without good reason could expect to be expelled or 'sent down', to quote the University's own terminology. Women were not admitted to the university until the 1900s and neither students or fellows were allowed to marry, thus thwarting any dreams Shakespeare had of attending Oxford, had he been so able or inclined.

The University at one time is known to have been suspicious of companies of players; they looked on actors as wild vagabonds and rogues, and over time players would be forced to seek noble patronage to give them an air of respectability. Shakespeare and his players rose to the very pinnacle of patronage, becoming the King's men, and records show that the King's men visited Oxford on many occasions. The most notable of these visits were May 1603, May–June 1604 and the King's players winter tour of 1605 and 1610[8]. From 1604 twelve members of the King's men had been appointed grooms of the chamber and Shakespeare was the driving force behind the plays. Oxford students lapped up plays such as *Hamlet* and *Romeo and Juliet*, as can be deduced from the worn pages of those plays in the Bodleian library's First Folio, whereas pages covering the tragedy of *King John* appear almost untouched.[9] Despite this evidence of acclaim, we know that the player/actor from Stratford's success wasn't always appreciated by the educated competition.

2. The Upstart

Over the centuries, the University's attitude towards Shakespeare has altered dramatically. Before his time, the only writers, apart from Thomas Kyd, with the assumed authority and perceived ability to write poetry and plays were the University wits, Oxford and Cambridge educated playwrights and pamphleteers, the late 16th century literary elite such as Thomas Nash, Ben Jonson and Christopher Marlowe. It is interesting to note that the first record of Shakespeare's rise to prominence is contained in a slanderous pamphlet written by the prolific playwright and poet Robert Greene. In 'Greene's Groats-worth of wit, bought with a million of repentance', Cambridge man Greene gives insight into the very real threat the uneducated Shakespeare brought to the playwright monopoly held by Greene and the Oxbridge elite. The pamphlet attacks the actor Shakespeare and his ambitious ilk as follows:

> *Yes, trust them not, for there is an upstart crow, beautified*
> *with our feathers, that, with his Tygers heart wrapt in a*
> *Players hide, supposes he is as well able to bumbast out*
> *a blanke verse as the best of you; and being an absolute*
> *Johannes Factotum, is in his owne conceit the onely Shake-*
> *scene in a countrie* [10]

Greene describes Shakespeare, or Shake-scene as he calls him, as an Upstart crow, having risen to prominence without the required qualifications and accused him of stealing the ideas of others, comparing him to a scavenging crow and that he was not a man to be trusted, implying that his motive was to put established writers out of commission. 'The tigers heart wrapt in a players hide', not only mocks the line from *Henry VI*, Part iii 'O tiger's heart wrapped in a woman's hide' but also implies that Shakespeare had malicious intent. Greene also calls him a Johannes factotum (Jack of all trades) in reference to the fact that he wrote as well as acted.

Whether Shakespeare intended to wipe out the established competition or not, you would be hard-pressed to find any works by Robert Greene studied in school or performed nowadays.

3. The Second Act Of Man

When Shakespeare's father fell on hard times, the once prominent Shakespeare family became very poor. In later years, following his success, William Shakespeare went to great lengths to procure a coat of arms for his family, which shows how much it meant for him to rise in status. Although this may have been born slightly from insecurity, witty ramblings from the likes of Robert Greene were unlikely to douse his ambition. Some speculate that the reason Shakespeare revealed himself first as an actor rather than a writer is because he wasn't University educated and was perhaps at first embarrassed.[11] I prefer the idea that he viewed his gift for writing as the next natural stage of his career evolution.

When looking through records concerning Shakespeare and his monetary dealings, it is clear that he was exceptionally shrewd. He lent money, hoarded malt as neighbours starved and took friends to court over petty debts.[12] Some of the surviving documentation on Shakespeare's life involve taking neighbours to court over paltry amounts when he himself could afford to purchase the largest properties in Stratford. Similarly, he was a man who became part of a conglomerate to build a theatre instead of hire one, only to then remove the entire building after squabbles with the landlord, and was known to write flattering poetry to seduce rich and noble patrons when plague made it impossible to perform to the public. He also had the intelligence and audacity to patch together old plays and rewrite them to suit actors, as only an actor could write, and thus cut out the established elite and the University wits. He was a hardnosed business man, sharp with a litigious streak and ruthlessly ambitious; there was no way he was going back to rock bottom again and the Oxbridge mob were never going put him in his place.

But how did Shakespeare, the bane of the literary hierarchy, become so successful, and what events in his childhood may have led to his treading of the boards? Shakespeare had plenty of opportunities to witness plays and to partake in performances throughout his youth, and like most Warwickshire lads would have grown up watching the Catholic morality plays, or mystery plays as they were also known. His father was, for a while, a prominent member of Stratford society, working his way up the ranks from Chief Ale Taster to eventually Mayor, which also would have given him greater exposure to travelling plays. This elevated position also entitled his sons to attend the local grammar school for free. So when sceptics point out Shakespeare's lack of university education they tend not to take into consideration how arduous grammar schools were, school days starting at 6am and finishing at 4pm.

The grammar school education in Shakespeare's time would have involved learning to read and write in Latin as well as English and would have prepared students to study Law and to be able to argue the case from both sides, a common trait in Shakespeare plays. For example, *Henry V* has both a joyous and sad ending depending on one's sympathies. Whether loyal to the king or to Falstaff, Shakespeare allows the audience to be judge and consider both perspectives. In addition, grammar school pupils would have participated in school plays to master their oration skills for a career in the pulpit or the law courts after University. Though he did not complete his education, we can safely assume he learned enough to serve him well in the future and that he developed a taste for acting at school fuelled by the players' visits, which would have entertained and inspired him.

Young Shakespeare would have also been only 100 miles from the best theatre London could offer. In 1569 the new phenomena of London's travelling acting troupes made their way to Stratford and performed in the Guildhall under the supervision of the Mayor, John Shakespeare, who had invited the Earl of Worcester's men and the Queen's men to play in the inn yards of the town. Over the next few years, ten acting troupes played Stratford: the Queens men came back three times; Worcester's another six times followed by Oxford's men, Warwick's men and the Earl of Essex's men.[13] But even if he had been exposed to plays in Stratford, how would an opportunity arise for Shakespeare to join an established acting troupe? The answer may lie with a bloody incident that occurred in the Oxfordshire town of Thame.

4. A Murder In Thame

The Queen's men were a travelling acting troupe of the highest order, formed around 1583 and sent around Britain to spread pro-Elizabethan propaganda. Of course, only the best actors of their generation could be entrusted to rouse the crowds with their patriotic stories, replete with bombastic speeches. This was an age of spymasters, religious upheaval and an insecure queen who, like Henry V, and more recently Margaret Thatcher, utilized victories abroad to paper over the cracks of dissatisfaction at home.

The troupe had the great fortune to have enlisted the most beloved comedian to ever grace a stage, Queen Elizabeth's favourite clown, Richard Tarlton. Tarlton's contribution to the world of drama should not be undervalued, and his popularity helped shape theatre into an entertainment for the masses, in a way, paving the way for the Shakespearian stage. The iconic image of the joker in a pack of playing cards is based on Tarlton,[14] such was his fame. In the volumes of 'Tarlton jests' manuscripts that were published just after the clown's death, a youthful talented player called William Knell is accredited in the role of Henry V. William Knell's stock must have soared in the mid-1580s as praise flowed years after from the usually acerbic playwright and critic Thomas Nashe. In his book Pierce Penniless, Nashe quipped that he would write a book in Latin on the achievements of Knell and his ilk so that they would surpass those of the ancient Roman actors. When the playwright Thomas Heywood wrote his essay 'An apology for actors' (1612) in defence against Puritan attacks, Knell's acting ability was again lauded.[15]

On the 13th June 1587 he took to the stage with the Queen's men in the market town of Thame, some nine miles from Oxford. Recently married to his fifteen-year old sweetheart, Rebecca Edwards, and now a leading light in England's greatest acting company, young William Knell had the world at his feet. Little could he have known that this midsummer's day would be his last. No one knows which play was performed that fateful day, but in the early evening after the performance, William Knell became embroiled in a furious row with one of his fellow actors, John Towne, the fracas probably taking place at The Spread Eagle inn, a public house that is still active today. Perhaps too much strong ale had been consumed, tempers possibly frayed by the constant lurching from one town to another; we will never know. The argument became so heated that Knell chased Towne into a close called the White Hound, swinging a sword at his fellow actor. Towne leapt onto a mound and in alleged self-defence struck at Knell. The sword thrust into Knells neck, creating a wound three inches deep and one inch wide, according to the coroner's report. Half an hour passed and the fire of youth had been extinguished; William Knell had bled to death. [16]

John Towne was eventually pardoned by the Queen due to claims that his violent reaction was self-defence. Even still, he must have been held in some esteem by his colleagues as he was reported as a Queen's man a decade later in 1597. Knell's young widow Rebecca inherited his estate and married a player who would become one of Shakespeare's closest friends, John Hemings.[17] We will never know if the unfortunate William Knell would have made more of an impact in the theatre world had his life not been cut short, but we do know that life goes on, and the Queen's men had the pressing task of playing the Oxfordshire market town of Abingdon the very next day, followed by a performance in Stratford upon Avon, but of course a man down! Some historians have speculated that young Shakespeare could have been just the man to step into the other William's shoes when the Queen's men visited his home town. It is a lovely notion, that being in the right place at the right time, the ambitious Shakespeare, well versed in literature and schooled in oratory, might have jumped at the chance to find a way out of the humdrum of daily life in a small and close-knit community.

The site of William Knell's death

If this tragic murder and subsequent vacancy in the troupe marked the beginning of Shakespeare's career with the Queen's men then it meant a life changing choice had to be made, leaving behind his wife and their three young children, Susanna and twins Judith and Hamnet. And if he had started out as an actor with the company at this time, it is generally assumed he then graduated to patching up the company's old plays such as *King Leir, The famous victories of Henry V, The troublesome reign of King John* and *The true tragedy of Richard III*, all of which are now associated within the Shakespeare canon![18]

Now back to reality. We believe that he progressed from the Queen's men in 1588 to Lord Strange's company, before a dalliance with Pembroke's men (1592–94), which led briefly to joining the players of Lord Sussex before a long tenure with the Lord Chamberlain's, comprised of both Admiral's and Strange's troupes, not long after the latter's death.[19] All the while climbing up the tower of influential and powerful patrons before reaching the pinnacle of royal patronage, a King's man. As rights to plays were owned by the playhouses as opposed to the author, the move from successful actor playwright and eventually a shareholder in his players company, was an astute move. Shakespeare became extremely successful and bought property back home in Stratford where he would return at intervals to visit his family and keep an eye on his various investments.

There were two possible routes from London to Stratford; both on treacherous roads and the journeys would have taken three to four days with nightly stopovers, approximately four days by foot, two to three days on horseback. To let loved ones know he was coming to visit, messages would have been passed on for a small fee by 'carriers', deliverers of goods such as cheese, mead and linen. Carriers would have been grateful for any extra monies as they were often targeted by thieves, though not for coinage, as deals were done on credit and exchange of goods. These goods would have been luxuries from London such as dates, almonds and rice, strangely then regarded as a spice and from Stratford, linen shirts, flaxseed oil and of course Cotswold wool. This was regarded as the best in Europe and a great magnet for roadside rogues,[20] perhaps not that dissimilar from canny Autolycus from The Winter's Tale. One route was by way of Aylesbury via Banbury, the other journey would have been the slightly quicker route via High Wycombe and then through Oxford. Here is a marvellous story that took place that suggests why Shakespeare may have preferred the Oxford route, for reasons other than a slightly quicker journey.

5. Much Ado In Grendon Underwood

'Grendon Underwood – the dirtiest town that ever stood.' These lines from an ancient Buckinghamshire rhyme sum up the state of the town's roads at the time of Shakespeare.[21] Luckily for current visitors, the roads have been improved incomparably to the poem's sentiment. The village was a thoroughfare from the northern realms of Oxfordshire, around twenty miles from Oxford city.

Shakespeare travelled through the beautiful Chiltern hills by way of Grendon Underwood on his way to Stratford upon Avon. A local legend is that Shakespeare often walked along the forest tracks, commonly frequented by gypsies and strolling players. Sometimes on his travels he would rest and stay the night at a large coaching inn which was called The Ship. The inn, now a private residence, was aptly renamed as Shakespeare's farm. It is a rather capacious Elizabethan construction, the gable with its oval window and large fireplace is rumoured to be the room in which Shakespeare slept and even worked on his plays. The original sign for the inn, which was established in 1570, is currently exhibited in the local museum. It's certainly a plausible location for him to have rested, though a cynic would say that he probably didn't spend enough time at the inn to actually work on plays, as the former hotel management cunningly suggested. There is also a tale that Shakespeare's ghost manifests on April 23rd (Shakespeare's birthday) of each year, peering out of a window on the top floor.[22]

A charming tale that crops up from his time spent in this idyllic setting involves an entertaining confrontation with the local police force. Shakespeare is reputed to have taken a nap on the porch of the local church, when he was abruptly awakened by two local constables who accused him of stealing items from the church. Upon being arrested, Shakespeare demanded to see the contents of the church trunk. When it became clear that nothing had been stolen and all was in order, Shakespeare apparently uttered the words 'Much ado about nothing'. The logic of the local constabulary leaves a lot to be desired, as its relatively unlikely that even the simplest of thieves would have gone to sleep at the scene of the crime. The dim-witted duo is reputed to have provided Shakespeare with inspiration for the two constables in *Much Ado About Nothing*,

Dogberry and Verges. [23]

    This tale is mentioned by the Oxford diarist, John Aubrey, who stated that the constables had the same humour as those in *Midsummer Night's Dream*. As often happens with Aubrey, his memory has let him down and he has evidently confused plays. We will never know nor be able to completely trust Aubrey's exact source who said that he actually heard the story first hand from one of the constables in 1642, still living in Grendon Underwood. My suspicion at first was that the story probably came from Aubrey's contemporary and friend William Davenant, a man whose family provide an important link with Shakespeare's Oxford visits. Before unfolding Davenant's story, let me tell you about a snack that Shakespeare might have eaten if he travelled the alternative route, via Banbury.

6. You Banbury Cheese!

On passing through the Oxfordshire town of Banbury, some twenty-one miles North of Oxford, it is possible that Shakespeare tasted one of the local delicacies, a yellow, strong smelling cow's milk cheese, called imaginatively, Banbury cheese, which dates back to at least 1594 and which he indeed references in the *Merry Wives of Windsor*. In Act 1, the rowdy Bardolph insults the slim frame of his acquaintance Slender by calling him a 'Banbury cheese'. It seems that the term Banbury cheese became popular slang for something uncommonly thin, as its also mentioned as an insult in Jack Drum's *Entertainment*, which reads 'You are like a Banbury cheese, nothing but paring!'[24] Though the Banbury cheese is preserved forever in literature, we will never know how it tasted as it is no longer commercially produced; perhaps its popularity dwindled due to its thin portions! So it is possible that Shakespeare may have decided to avoid run-ins with the Buckingham constabulary by going via Oxford, even if it meant missing out on Banbury's famous cheese.[25]

    But when he arrived in Oxford where did he stay and with whom?

7. The Painted Room

The 13th century Carfax tower, formerly part of St Martin's, the official city church at the time of Shakespeare's life, is positioned at the crossroads of Oxfords four central streets and sits very close to the place where it is thought that Shakespeare stayed when he visited Oxford, a public house called the Crown Inn. Just less than a minute's walk north of the tower today you will see a place called the Crown public house tucked down a path off Cornmarket Street. Many have thought this must be the Crown Inn where Shakespeare stayed on his travels. However, this is incorrect and a plaque on the wall actually states that he did not reside there, which I think is a refreshingly honest admission during these competitive times for drinking establishments in England! In Shakespeare's day the Crown Inn was actually known as The King's Head inn and punters would come to watch plays that were performed in the courtyard. On this basis, it is highly likely that Shakespeare would have known and visited the inn. However, the Crown Inn where it is claimed that Shakespeare may have stayed is actually on the opposite side of the street from the public house that now has this name.

    Number 3 Cornmarket, home to the former Crown Inn, sits near to the location of another historic inn, the Golden Cross, which today is remembered by the courtyard of the same name. A few winding wooden steps above an ordinary book-makers, next to what is now a café, lead to a hidden treasure of a room which would have been part of the Crown Inn and contains remarkably well preserved 16th century wall paintings. The beautiful wall paintings display inexact textile patterns of entwining bright flowers.[26] The decorative imagery may seem bold to modern eyes but would have been more familiar to the original householders, reminiscent of old church wall paintings and stain glass windows which often employed colourful imagery to convey religious parables to a predominantly illiterate parish.

From 1564 to 1581 this Crown Inn was called Tattleton's, named after a tailor who lived there during this period and it is thought he may have commissioned the paintings, as his initials were discovered in one of the adjoining rooms, later demolished. His stepchildren, who inherited the tenancy, may have thought the wall paintings an eyesore, as by 1594 a New College inventory shows the paintings had been covered with wainscoting.[27] Curiously, there are two sets of texts from different faiths on adjacent walls that evoke the religious upheaval of the times. Above a fireplace, the monogram of Jesus, IHS, very much a symbol associated with Catholicism and with the Jesuits, which would have been a dangerous statement to retain on the wall in Elizabethan times and probably dates back to the reign of her sister, Queen Mary. Running along the top of the flowery patterns we have the following moral message that sounds more Protestant.

'first of thi rising, and last of thi rest by thou, Gods servant that hold I best, in the morning early, serve God Devoutlie, fear God above Allthynge, honour the Kynge'

This is the room that Shakespeare is rumoured to have stayed in, as a guest and friend of the family who ran the inn, the Davenants.

John Davenant was, like his father before him, a wine merchant and middleman broker.[28] He lived in London with his wife Jane, or Jennet, as she was also known. The records of St James Garlickhythe in London, paint a sombre picture of the first five years of their marriage. Their first five offspring were buried between Christmas 1593 and Christmas 1597, either stillborn or dying very young. A desperate Jane sought the counsel of the infamous quack doctor and stargazer Simon Foreman. Foreman stated 'she supposeth herself with child, but it is not so!' yet another child died in 1599.[29] It is thought that the couple may have headed to Oxford to seek a cleaner atmosphere; if this was the case they were extremely fortunate – all seven of the children Jane bore in Oxford survived.

The Oxford-educated poet John Donne and his family may have also been somewhat instrumental in the Davenant's move to Oxford. John Donne's London home in Bread Street was a stone's throw from the Davenant's household and he and Davenant were known to attend plays often. Davenant, was a 'lover of playes and playmakers' (Wood) and Donne 'a great frequenter of playes' to quote sir Richard Baker. Donne's aunt lived in Oxford and her husband Robert Dawson was a vintner at the Blue Boar on St. Aldates. Donne matriculated at Hart Hall (now Hereford college) the year his aunt died, and her husband Robert remarried and continued at the Blue Boar. When Dawson passed away in 1605, Donne's cousins and friends Edward and Grace Dawson took over the tenure. The Blue Boar was just a minute's walk from the Crown Inn, and with both inns being tenants of New College, the Davenant and Donne families would have once again been neighbours, as they had been in

London. Donne may not have been the only poet to influence a move to Oxford,[30] and perhaps Shakespeare who also knew them both may well have had a hand. Under what circumstances did Shakespeare know the Davenants?

There are a few plausible connections. Jane Davenant's brother, Thomas Sheppard, was a court embroider and glover. He embroidered black cloth for the mourning livery of Queen Elizabeth's funeral and was the official designated perfumer for King James, which must have been a difficult task, as famously the King had taken but one bath his entire life! Shakespeare and Thomas Sheppard were employed by court at the same time and it is therefore a realistic supposition that Shakespeare, the glove-maker's son may have taken an interest in Sheppard's trade. Another link is that Thomas Sheppard's son, Robert, was also employed by the court as a King's messenger. There is also a professional connection between Thomas Sheppard and Shakespeare's Cripplegate landlady, Marie Mountjoy. Marie was a maker of headdressers for Queen Anne and Thomas Sheppard was the Queen's glove maker. In addition, the Davenant's London residence was in a parish directly opposite the Bankside theatres.[31]

It is crucial to stress that in Oxford, John Davenant was the landlord of the Crown Inn, not the Crown Tavern. The difference between an inn and a wine tavern is that the latter were basically the drinking holes and common rooms of the university. This means that Shakespeare would have lodged at the Crown Inn as a guest, a friend of the family, not paying board. A New College manuscript informs that all three of the Cornmarket properties they leased, the Inn, a tavern and a tenement between them, were, in the 1590s, in the hands of a family called Underhill, stepchildren of Tattleton the tailor and also distant relatives of the man who sold New Place in Stratford to Shakespeare.[32] With this Stratford connection in mind it is not too bold an assumption that Shakespeare stayed at the Crown Inn during the Underhill tenure. It is also likely that Shakespeare knew the Davenants from their days in London and may well have advised John to take over the Crown Inn, knowing that the current wine merchant Pierce Underhill was old and struggling to run the popular establishment after his sister Joan had left to marry in London, leaving him to run the place alone.[33]

We cannot be sure of the exact arrival of the Davenants but their first Oxford reference dates to the 11th February 1602, the baptism of their second daughter, Jane at St Martin's church at Carfax.[34] Legends surround Shakespeare's relationship with the Davenant's that have provoked much controversy and provided saucy material aplenty for romantic novelists over the centuries. In particular Shakespeare's rumoured affair with Jane Davenant, some say the woman perhaps most romantically linked historically to Shakespeare apart from his wife. There is also the Oxford tradition that Shakespeare was not just Godfather to one of their children, William Davenant, but in fact the father. This Oxford tradition is supported by two of William Davenant's contemporaries, the infamous gossips, antiquarians and friends Anthony Wood and John Aubrey, two biographers who never shied from introducing their own prejudices into their writings. Their works have, however, given us a priceless insight into the social mechanisms of early 17th century Oxford.

Wood was born in December 1632 and studied at Merton College after his education was disrupted by the English civil war. His most accomplished work was on the History of Oxford University which appeared in 1674, his *Historia, et antiquitaries Universitatis Oxoniensis*. His erstwhile partner in antiquity, Aubrey, six years his junior, also had his education (Trinity college) stilted by the war, though respected in the field of archaeology, fame came Aubrey's way from his *Brief Lives, a History of Poets, Scientists and other leading contemporary figures*, an incredibly entertaining read which I highly recommend, with a few pinches of salt!

It is from Aubrey and Wood that this Oxford tradition is initially regaled. Aubrey wrote

> *His [Sir William Davenant's] father was John Davenant, a Vintner there, a very grave and discreet Citizen; his mother was a very beautifull woman, and of a very good witt, and of conversation extremely agreable. They had three sons, viz. 1, Robert, 2, William, and 3, Nicholas (an attorney): and two handsome daughters, one married to Gabriel Bridges (B. D, fellow of C. C. Coll, beneficed in the Vale of White Horse), another to Dr. (William) Sherburne (minister of Pembridge in Hereford, and a canon of that church). Mr William Shakespeare was wont to goe into Warwickshire once a yeare, and did commonly in his journey lye at this house in Oxon. where he was exceedingly respected. [I have heard parson Robert (Davenant) say that Mr. W. Shakespeare has given him a hundred kisses.] Now Sir William would sometimes, when he was pleasant over a glass of wine with his most intimate friends — say, that it seemed to him that he wrote with the very spirit that Shakespeare wrote, and seemed contented enough to be thought his son. (He would tell them the story as above, in which way his mother had a very light report.)*[35]

Aubrey's description of John Davenant's sad demeanour was corroborated by Wood Davenant's sad demeanour.

> *John Davenant was a sufficient vintner, kept the tavern now known by the name of the Crowne, … was mayor of the said city in the year 1621, … was a very grave and discreet citizen (yet an admirer of plays and play-makers, especially Shakespeare, who frequented his house in his journies between Warwickshire and London), was of a melancholic disposition, and was seldome or never known to laugh.*[36]

According to the gossips, William Davenant didn't mind denigrating his Mother's reputation and is thought to have on occasion whilst inebriated insinuated that he was the son of Shakespeare. Perhaps he made this bold claim to further his own career as a playwright, maybe he meant son as in the way the followers of Ben Jonson were called the sons of Jonson, or perhaps he simply believed he was Shakespeare's son. Though Wood and Aubrey didn't mind offending people, they did know the Davenants very well and often drank at their establishment, the Crown.

After John Davenant and his wife died, the Crown came to be run by their daughter Jane who in turn housed two of her brother William's offspring, young Mary and William.

William Davenant's baptism by Tanya Dempsey

Sir Williams brother, Nicholas Davenant, the attorney, worked for Anthony Wood. This also means that they had plenty of time to talk with the Davenant family on these subjects.

These rumours were publicised well after William Davenant's death. Oxford scholar of St Edmund Hall, Thomas Hearne, who was also a Bodleian library assistant keeper and antiquarian, was only three years old when William Davenant passed away in 1668 and didn't reach Oxford till 1696 yet was clearly aware of the Oxford tradition stating 'Mr Shakespeare was his father and gave him his name.' To which Hearne added "Tis further said, that one day going from school, a grave doctor in Divinity met him and asked him "Child, whether thou art going in such haste?" to which the child replyed, "O, sir, my God-father is come to town, and I am going to ask his blessing." To which the Dr said, "Hold, child! You must not take the name of God in vaine"."
To gain a better understanding of the controversial relationship between Shakespeare and the Davenants let's probe more deeply into the characters of the Davenant family members. [37]

8. Jaques Of Oxford

Tradition has it that Ben Jonson was the role model for Jaques, perhaps Shakespeare's most melancholy character, one who could suck melancholy out of a song as in *As you like it*.[38] That may well have been a tit for tat dig at Jonson for lampooning the efforts Shakespeare went to achieve his family coat of arms. In *Every man in his humour*[39] Jonson mocks the ambition of fools spending their entire savings to procure their family a coat of arms. When Shakespeare coined his family motto 'not without right', Jonson gave Sogliardo the motto 'not without mustard'[40]. Another possible candidate to provide inspiration for Jaques could have been Shakespeare's friend and Oxford Vintner, John Davenant. As stated by Aubrey and Wood, John Davenant was a 'grave and discreet citizen' and 'was of a melancholic disposition, and was seldome or never known to laugh'. Perhaps the death of his first five offspring may have contributed to his solemn disposition, or perhaps it was just his natural demeanour. He certainly wouldn't be the first or last moody pub landlord that's poured pints in Oxford!

Davenant's move to Oxford brought him a great deal of status. He achieved a bailiff's place on the council on 4th June 1604 and shortly afterwards he was awarded one of the three city licences to sell wine, eventually rising in social status to become Mayor of Oxford in 1621.[41] He was also 'an admirer of plays and play-makers, especially Shakespeare'. Though John Davenant's London residence was the national hub of theatre, Oxford was teeming with visiting companies and his various roles within local politics would enable grand opportunities to witness high class theatre. As mentioned before, the galleried King's Head Inn directly opposite the Crown often hosted plays in their inn yard, performed by lodging player companies. The earliest audiences for Shakespeare's *Hamlet* were in the Oxbridge University cities around 1602-03, hardly surprising when one considers how popular the play about the troubled scholar Hamlet was amongst England's students.[42]

It could be that the stress of being Mayor, with all the unpaid work that came with that title, may have taken its toll on John Davenant, as he died on 19th April, less than a year after becoming Mayor. Though it is more likely he died of a broken heart, for the man who naturally suffered a melancholy nature died just fourteen days after the passing of his beautiful wife Jennet.[43] Two anonymous poems discovered many years later in the Earl of Warwick's library give curious tributes to John Davenant.

Poem 1 MR DAVENANT

If to bee greate or good deserve the baies,
What merits hee whom greate and good doth praise?
What meritts hee ? Why, a contented life,
A happy issue of a vertuous wife,
The choice of freinds, a quiet honour'd grave, All these hee
had; What more could Dav'nant have ?
Reader, go home, and with a weeping eye, For thy sins past,
learne thus to live and die.

Poem 2

Why Should hee dye?
And yet why should he live, his mate being gone,
And Turtle like sigh out an endless moone?
No, no, he loved her better, and would not
So easely lose what hee so hardly got
He liv'd to pay the last rites to his bride
That done, hee pin'd out fourteen days and died[44]

The acknowledgement of the short timeframe between John and his wife's death, alludes to a poet who knew the Davenants rather well. The strange wording of 'would not so easily lose what he so hardly got' fans the flames that there may have been an indifference from Jennet.

Davenant road, named after the former Mayor

9. The Dark Lady Of Oxford – Jennet Davenant

Shakespeare and The inn keepers wife by Alex singleton

Jane Davenant was born in London 1568 and would have been in her early thirties by the time she reached Oxford, as mentioned before, a move perhaps instigated by five failed pregnancies, a want for cleaner air and less polluted water, far from London's overcrowded Southbank. Their Oxford days were a much happier period and, as stated earlier, Jane gave birth seven times successfully.

Over the last four centuries, authors of biographies and fiction have often brought Jane Davenant into the fold as a lover of Shakespeare. Jane is usually described as a beautiful, witty woman, unlike Shakespeare's wife, Anne Hathaway who has seldom ever been described in a positive light, unfairly and without any justification it must be said[45]. And it is the painted room of the then Crown, which is often assumed as the romantic love nest of passion for the landlady and poet. This notion is brought up in two biographies, Schoenbaum's *Shakespeare lives* (1970)[46] and in Nethercot's *William Shakespeare* (1938) in which a photograph of the painted room is used as the front cover. In Sir Walter Scott's historical novel, *Woodstock* (1826) Jane Davenant is presented as 'the good looking, laughing, buxom hostess of an inn between Stratford and London'. In Ovid Kent's relatively recent novel, *Shakespeare is missing* (2013)[47] Jane is mentioned as the 'dark lady of the sonnets'. George Bernard Shaw, in retrospect, regretted that he did not choose Jane Davenant over Queen Elizabeth's maid of honour Mary Fitton, as the temptress in his short comic play, *The Dark lady of the Sonnets* (1908). Not only did Jane's son, William, claim to be Shakespeare's bastard son, but his brother Robert said he himself received a hundred kisses from the esteemed family friend. It is not inconceivable that sombre John, the landlord may have been more involved in the administrative side of running the tavern, as well as busying himself with local government, and the attractive Jane was the face of the tavern. Perhaps her beauty became something of local fame amongst the Oxford drinkers in the small city.[48] That, coupled with the personable nature of a tavern hostess, may have got the gossip's chins wagging, and it didn't take much to get Wood and Aubrey started! Having a celebrated playwright as a regular guest would only add fuel to the fire. There was even a novella published in 1594 by an Oxford student that I am amazed has received scant attention in the field of Shakespearean biography. *Willobie His Avisa*, a mysterious book which not only parodies Venus and Adonis but also references *The Rape of Lucrece*, corroborates the Jane Davenant affair and brings to life the sonnet's love triangle. More significantly it gives the world the first mention of Shakespeare in literature.

10. The Poet, The Scholar And The Innkeeper's Wife

On 3rd September 1594 the Novella, *Willobie his Avisa*, was licensed for the press by printer John Windet, a man who specialised in printing sheet music. It was attributed to an Oxford student called Henry Willobie who, at sixteen years old, matriculated at St John's college 10th December 1591 and went onto graduate with a Bachelor of Arts from Exeter college in 1595, around six months after his novella was published. The book was printed again on 30th June 1596, this time published after the young author Willobie was reported dead. This posthumous edition was published with an 'Apologie' by a friend of the late author, Hadrian Dorell, who had gone to the trouble to have Willobie's book reprinted. Dorrel explains in his epistle that Willobie's papers were left as his responsibility whilst his friend left Oxford voluntarily on her majesty's service to see 'the fashions of other countries', and that he was 'now of late gone to God'. He also states that he had found the manuscript amongst Willobie's belongings.[49]

The book tells the tale of an exceptionally beautiful woman by the name of Avisa, who after turning down the advances of a noble man, marries an innkeeper (sounds familiar). She then has to fend off the amorous ambitions of five more suitors. The other five that pursue the married inn keeper are a Cavaleiro, a Frenchman, Dudum Beatus Dydimus Harco, Anglo-Germanus, W.S., an old player and Henrico Willobego Italio Hispalensis, a Italian twist on the authors name. Though some of the names are clearly in jest, they seem to represent English men who fashioned their love-making on foreign national stereotypes. The 'old player' W.S., who has also been rebuffed by Avisa the 'vertuos' lady, offers advice to the young student, depicting Avisa as perhaps not so Chaste with lines such as

> *Apply her still with dyvers things*
> *(for gifts the wisest will deceive)*
> *Some times with gold, sometimes with*
> *No tyme nor fit occasion leave*
> *Though coy at first she seeme and weilde*
> *These toyes in tyme wil make her yield*[50]

Alas, all the besotted admirers are turned down by the innkeeper's wife. There are two poems in the 1594 preface, one of which contains the following lines, which add further validation that the W.S. of the Novella is meant to be Shakespeare, 'the old player' and 'familiar friend' character in the story. 'Yet Tarquyne pluckt his glistering grape, and Shake-speare paints poore Lucrece rape.' Shakespeare's highly successful *The Rape of Lucrece* was printed only four months earlier and this is the first ever independent reference to Shakespeare in literature.[51] The fog of mystery thickens further when it becomes clear that no one by the name of Hadrian Dorrel has been documented as an Oxford student, which leads us to think that it was a pseudonym.

The novella was extremely popular and often reprinted, going through six editions, printed even as late as 1635. It was, however, banned in 1596 by the Bishop of London and again by the supreme censor, the Archbishop of Canterbury, with an order that all copies be burned in 1599.[52] Someone in power was clearly unhappy with a hinted portrayal within the novella.

Nevertheless, the success of *Avisa* was such that it even inspired imitation, notably Mathew Roydon's *Penelope's complaint* in which Royden made no attempt to hide his source of inspiration, even praising the novella in his own preface.[53] It is unclear how the alleged author Willobie died whilst on 'her majesty's service'. Though not exactly a training ground for Elizabethan spies, Exeter college did produce a few, including the college rector John Neale in the 1570s, and it is possible Willobie may well have been killed during a mission in Italy or France, or perhaps at the great Battle of Gran in Hungary against the Turks (Aug 1595).[54] Or he may have met his demise from a party offended by the book. After all these were dangerous times to publicly mock or undermine people in the public eye. Though the real identities of the suitors are a mystery to modern audiences, Elizabethan readers may well have been in the know, their identities perhaps commonplace gossip. Important records, plays and manuscripts have been lost over the centuries and so it would be of no surprise if pamphlets existed which commentated on the real life identities of the suitors.

So we have a story, with some disguised members vying for the attentions of a glamorous innkeeper's wife, in which the alleged young author Henry Willobie makes an appearance, strong hints of personal connections to Shakespeare and numerous early references to his most popular poems. There is also a moral phrase on the front page of the 1594 publication that caught my eye, Proverb 12.4 which may have been a subtle reference to the name of the public house in which worked the Chaste wife, 'A vertuous woman is the Crown of her husband'. *Avisa* was written at least a decade before the birth of William Davenant, so if Jane Davenant gave birth to a son named William, Shakespeare's Godson, and so if Shakespeare was actually father, the affair may have lasted quite some time.

Now let's look into the extraordinary life of the Oxford playwright who himself claimed to be the son of Shakespeare.

11. William Davenant, Bastard Son Of Shakespeare

William Davenant's life was a dramatic ride that one couldn't script. Fighting heroically in wars, imprisonment, gun running and achieving great triumphs in the world of theatre. His roles in both the English Civil War and the world of drama are somewhat overlooked.

Sir William Davenant was born in February 1606 and even as a child he displayed a real zest for writing poetry. Like his older brother Robert, he studied at Oxford, the latter at St John's whilst William studied at Lincoln. His studies, however, were cut short suddenly upon the death of his father, when he withdrew from college before having the chance to take a degree. It is thought that William had enjoyed university life and, according to Anthony A. Wood, he 'wanted much of university learning' and it was around this period Wood described the poet as 'The Sweet swan of Isis', a term that evokes the nickname Ben Jonson bestowed upon Shakespeare, 'The sweet swan of Avon'.

An opportunity arose for young William to appear at court as Page to the Duchess of Richmond, which subsequently led to his employment with Fulke Greville, Lord Brooke, until the Lord was stabbed to death by a servant in 1628. Whilst under the service of Lord Brooke, Davenant began working on plays, the first of which, *The Cruel brother*, licensed on 12 January 1626, was a success and was performed by the King's servants at Blackfriars.[55] His second play was, however, not so popular. The bloody *Albovine* received little exposure during his lifetime though was performed at his old Oxford college by the Davenant society, 300 years later in 1931![56]

Will Davenant by Jon Patterson

Out of work following the unfortunate death of Lord Brooke, Davenant turned the crisis into an opportunity and took to writing for the stage full time, becoming the most successful Oxford-born playwright and theatre manager. Davenant's writing was often interrupted by war and his early career as a courtier led to his first stint in military service. In 1627 Davenant accompanied the inept and crass George Villiers, the Duke of Buckingham, in his disastrous Siege of Saint Martin de Re, a battle which involved English Protestants fighting against French Protestants in aid of Cardinal Richelieu, the chief French minister, much to the horror of parliament. The following year Buckingham, in a complete U turn, supported the Huguenots he had previously attacked, against the Cardinal whom he suspected of treachery. This war led to losing over one half of the 7,000 English soldiers deployed; Davenant was one of the fortunate survivors. Around the time he suffered terribly from venereal disease in 1630, his play *The Just Italian* was being performed by the company associated with Shakespeare, the King's men.

From his mid-twenties he was often cruelly mocked for his appearance, having experienced a gross disfigurement of his nose from mercury treatment after he 'gott a terrible clap of a black handsome wench that lay in Axe-yard Westminster', to quote Aubrey. Some would say he was fortunate only to lose his nose as many had lost their lives to syphilis, or the grand pox as it was then known. One cruel commentator joked that 'his art was high, though his nose was low'. During his recovery Davenant actually stabbed a man with a rapier for laughing at his disfigurement. The victim, Thomas Warren, died shortly after the attack. Davenant then fled to Holland to escape conviction but was pardoned by King Charles, a reprieve probably largely due to his military service with the previous monarch's favourite, Buckingham.[57] 1630 was the same year in which Blackfriars restaged Davenant's successful play, *The Cruel Brother*.

During this period, the Court Masques were exceptionally important political social events. The artistic components of the Masques were entrusted for many years to the ingenious duo, Inigo Jones and Ben Jonson. Jonson's literary reputation was such that he stood as sole champion of writing verses for the masques and Inigo Jones was let loose to work visual magic on the sets, effects and stage designs. Though the pair complemented each other as artists, at least in the eyes of the audiences, they didn't gel personally and their working relationship fell apart in 1634. Their fallout led the way for Jones to work with a younger poet, William Davenant, who seized this opportunity with great aplomb. Davenant was not a difficult personality, unlike the ageing Jonson, and proceeded to write the remaining Caroline Masques including the popular *Temple of love* and the *Triumphs of the Prince D'amour*. By the time he was in his twenties he had a resume of seven full-length plays. Around this hectic period, Davenant managed to publish his first collection of 43 poems, *Madagascar*. When Jonson died, Davenant was unofficially acknowledged as the heir apparent, the royal poet laureate, a position he held unchallenged until his death, three decades later. [58]

Unfortunately, war was again just round the corner, and there was no sitting on the fence for the court poet who stood firmly with King Charles. In the spring of 1641, Davenant was embroiled in a failed attempt to set the army against parliament. The 'Army plot', as it was called, was regarded by some puritans as the greatest treason discovered since the Gunpowder plot. Davenant was named alongside Sir John Suckling, Mr Percy, and Mr Jermyn, amongst other conspirators, as having fled.[59] On 2nd September, 1642, Cromwell's puritan parliament made an enemy out of all playwrights and actors and banned plays. In 1649, two months after the King's death, Cromwell's soldiers smashed the interiors of England's theatres.[60] Shakespeare must have been turning in his grave!

Davenant was an extremely active Royalist during the English Civil War and he became Queen Henrietta Maria's aide and close friend. The Queen recommended him to be Lieutenant General of the Ordnance after pawning royal jewels in Amsterdam at her behest. He went on to act as gunrunner, supplying arms to Royalist forces in the west of England, boldly gunrunning through Parliament blockades! His bravery was rewarded and King Charles knighted him for his daring actions. [61]

The revolution, however, was eventually achieved by Cromwell and, after the King was beheaded, Davenant was exiled in France alongside his friend Henrietta Marie and her son, Prince Charles. Whilst away from England, Davenant had the time to begin writing his epic poem, *Gondibert*,[62] however, his efforts were cut short by way of a promotion as he was appointed Lieutenant Governor of Maryland. This move proved to be an almighty set back as he was captured on arrival by English troops, brought back to England and imprisoned in the Tower of London where he narrowly escaped death, twice on trial for being an enemy of the commonwealth. He languished in the dreaded tower for a miserable year in 1651. At least he managed to finish writing *Gondibert*![63]

Upon his release in 1652, Davenant learned quickly that the life of a playwright was going to be difficult under Cromwell's rule. With plays banned and theatres demolished, Davenant came up with a series of genius innovations to bypass the puritan bans. He bought Rutland House on New Charterhouse Square, London, which he turned into a private theatre[64] and in 1656 he introduced to England the first English opera, *The Siege of Rhodes*. He also brought to the stage England's first professional actress, Catherine Coleman. Davenant divided the musical into five acts from the standard three to further differentiate it from plays. He brought under his wing one of the greatest 17th century composers, Matthew Locke. Entry to Davenant's new style of private theatre cost five shillings per head. Davenant's next cunning move was to compose anti-Spanish 'Operas', during a period of strong ill feeling towards the Spanish from the Puritan rulers. Davenant used this move to establish himself as the manager of the Cock Pit theatre, Drury Lane, where he introduced the world to theatre drapes. [65]

During the Restoration, Davenant and his one serious rival, Thomas Killigrew, enjoyed royal patronage, Davenant enjoyed that of the King's brother, the Duke of York and the future King James II. With this Royal patronage Davenant founded the Duke's company.[66] It was this time when Shakespeare was not in vogue that Davenant insisted on the exclusive rights to perform Shakespeare's works.[67] As Shakespeare's troupe had boasted the greatest actor of their period, Richard Burbage, Davenant had the great fortune to work with the Burbage of his era, Thomas Betterton, a man Samuel Pepys viewed as the greatest actor in the world.[68] In 1708 The bookkeeper for Davenant's company, John Downes, made an insightful connection between Shakespeare's stage directions for *Hamlet* and Davenant's when he wrote 'Sir William (having seen Mr Taylor of the Black-Fryars company act it, who being instructed by the author Mr Shaksepeur) taught Mr Betterton in every particle of it, which by of his exact performance of it, gain'd him Esteem and Reputation, superlative to all other plays.'[69] Thomas Betterton would play Hamlet right up to his mid-seventies, until riddled with gout he gave his last performance in 1709, the same year he had journeyed to Stratford upon Avon to glean information from the locals for Nicholas Rowe's seminal Shakespeare biography. During this period Davenant introduced the world to innovations that set the template for the modern stage, he gave us theatre curtains, the classic proscenium arch stage with doors allowing access to the stage, moveable painted scenery and a scene store.[70]

Though Davenant was criticised for his excessive cutting of Shakespeare's works,[71] especially his mish-mash of *Much ado* and *Measure for measure*, it is ironic that Davenant was the only theatre manager for centuries to produce *King Lear* with Shakespeare's original miserable ending. It wouldn't be until the 19th century that directors would restore the ending. Other Davenant adaptations of Shakespeare included *The Rivals*, an updated version of *The Two Noble Kinsmen*, and a spectacular, high budget version of *Henry VIII*.[72] Perhaps the most loved was Davenant's collaboration with John Dryden, an operatic version of The Tempest called *The Enchanted Island.* [73]

When Davenant died on 7th April 1668 he had left behind a fantastic legacy to both the development of modern theatre and to the continued performance of Shakespeare's works, at a time when they were viewed as outdated. He was buried near Chaucer's Monument with an engraving that evokes Ben Jonsons epitaph, 'O Rare Sir William Davenant'. [74]

As Aubrey mentioned, Davenant didn't mind telling his friends that he was actually Shakespeare's son, over a glass of wine. Whether he actually believed this to be true, we will never know. However, we can say with certainty that 'the sweet swan of Isis' was clearly affected by Shakespeare's life and death. In 1618, at the tender age of twelve he composed this touching memorial poem.

ODE IN REMBRANCE OF MASTER SHAKESPEARE

Beware, delighted poets, when you sing,
To welcome nature in the early spring,
Your numerous feet not tread
The banks of Avon, for each flower
(As it ne'er knew a sun or shower)
Hangs there the pensive head.

Each Tree, whose thick, and spreading growth hath made,
Rather a Night beneath the Boughs, than Shade,
(Unwilling now to grow)
Looks like the Plume a Captive wears,
Whose rifled Falls are steeped i'th tears
Which from his last rage flow.

The piteous River wept itself away
Long since (Alas!) to such a swift decay;
That reach the Map; and look
If you a River there can spy;
And for a River your mock'd Eye,
Will find a shallow Brook. [75]

Regardless of the love child rumours, it is clear that Davenant was deeply affected by Shakespeare's death at a young age, If Shakespeare did witness the baptism of William Davenant as Godfather, the original Font used for that ceremony now resides in the City Church of St Michael's at the Northgate, less than a minute's walk North from the painted room.

We can fairly deduce from Davenant's faithful allegiance to the Royal family, especially to Queen Henrietta Marie, that he was a Catholic sympathiser. Near the end of his rollercoaster life he converted to Roman Catholicism, the old religion of England, which had been persecuted since the reign of Queen Elizabeth. That brings us neatly to an ancient Oxford college which has seen its fair share of religious led executions as well as the kindling of infamous regicidal plots.

12. If The Walls Of Balliol Could Talk

Balliol college is one of the very oldest University establishments, dating back to 1263, steeped in violent history, religious turmoil and assassination plots. Even the foundation of Balliol is unique, stemming from an argument over land between the King of Scotland's father, John De Balliol and the Bishop of Durham. The Bishop won the dispute and De Balliol, after being whipped, was forced as a penance to establish a house of study for sixteen poor scholars on a cheap plot of land outside the city walls, and thus Balliol college was founded. Though John De Balliol died not long after its foundation, his extraordinary wife took over his duties, writing the statutes and ensuring the future of Oxford's oldest college. She displayed her devotion to her husband in a way that can only be described as romantically macabre, as she carried her late husband's heart in a tiny casket she wore around her neck on a chain. The bizarre beginnings of this college would set the scene for centuries of strange and monumental events.

In 1555, when Queen Mary attempted to restore the country back to Catholicism, after the destructive reformation introduced by her father, Henry VIII and continued by her short lived brother Edward VI, she would do so with great gusto. Over three hundred high-profile Protestants were burnt to death in Smithfield Square London, before she targeted those even higher up the echelons of protestant clergy, including two Bishops, Latimer and Ridley and the Archbishop of Canterbury, Thomas Cranmer who were burnt to death for their perceived heresy to the crown, directly outside Balliol college. In fact, a former front door, which now leads to the college garden, still bares scorch marks from the fire which consumed the Bishops.

When Elizabeth was monarch all changed again and the established religion became the Church of England, and it was soon illegal and highly dangerous to be a practising Catholic. Nevertheless, Catholicism was the traditional religion of England and many were determined to fight against the laws encroaching upon their faith, by any means. This religious persecution was the backdrop to the life of a fervently Catholic Balliol man, a priest who organised many attempts on the Virgin Queen's life and had a number of connections with Shakespeare, the Jesuit Robert Parsons.

13. He Died A Papist

To gather a better understanding of Shakespeare, it is essential to look at both the extremely dangerous times he lived through and the faith which enveloped his upbringing. These were times in which following the wrong religion at the wrong time was dependent was highly dangerous and at the whim of whichever monarch happened to be in power and the influential whispers of the privy council. Shakespeare's family background was Catholic. His childhood home of Stratford upon Avon was a rural community, 100 miles from the capital and the monarch's protestant policies in London. Approximately thirty Catholic families lived in the small Stratford town who were likely close business colleagues. Trade deals were often hammered out in taverns and the popular Angel Inn was run by the passionately Catholic Cawdrey family, one of which was an exiled Jesuit priest. Shakespeare's mother, Mary Arden, was related to the infamous Ardens of Park Hall, her older relative, Margaret Arden of Park Hall married the Catholic renegade John Somerville.[76]

On 25th October 1583, Somerville, either drunk, insane or perhaps both, told anyone who would listen that he was determined to assassinate Queen Elizabeth. Warwickshire and the Arden family would not have known what hit them as government agents arrested John Somerville the day after his boasts. The agents then swooped on Park Hall, arrested Somerville's brother Francis, his friend, Hugh Hall, his wife Margaret and even her poor parents, Edward and Mary Arden. the Tower of London was their next destination. All were pardoned apart from Edward Arden and John Somerville whose plea of insanity was thrown out. John hung himself on the eve of his execution, his head was placed on a spike next to his father-in-law's. [77]

Two of Shakespeare's ancestors on his father's side were at one stage prioresses of a local nunnery in the 1500s, and George Badger, a neighbour of the Shakespeare family and a colleague of John Shakespeare, was imprisoned for his Catholic faith. Four of Shakespeare's schoolmasters at King's New School were Catholics. They included Simon Hunt, who later became a Jesuit priest and Thomas Jenkins, Hunt's successor who would have known both Robert Parsons and the Martyr Edmund Campion at Oxford. Jenkins was a student of the latter at St. John's college, and school master John Cottam whose brother, Jesuit priest Thomas, was hung at Tyburn for his faith.[78]

As for Shakespeare himself, it was noted by some of his peers that he didn't compose a tribute to the recently deceased Queen Elizabeth, as many of the renowned poets of the day had done. Similarly Shakespeare's plays are awash with banished characters, exiled like the Jesuit priests. There is also a theory that Shakespeare cloaked the identity of his political feelings by setting stories abroad, often in Italy, a location clearly synonymous with Catholicism. The clearest indication that Shakespeare was Catholic are within a series of biographical notes on Shakespeare, including a miscellany of manuscripts kept in the archives of Oxford's Corpus Christi college since 1689, compiled by two of Shakespeare's Warwickshire contemporaries, predominantly by William Fulman and his friend, the Reverend Richard Davies. William Fulman spent most of his life collating rare documents which he left to the Reverend in 1688, to complete unfinished points and present to Fulman's old college, Corpus Christi. Former Oxford student Richard Davies (Christ Church) had been the Vicar of Sapperton, not far from Stratford upon Avon. Six volumes of their collaborative works concentrated on religious and civil history and eleven volumes concerned Oxford University and then miscellaneous information on poets, which comprise the remaining eight volumes. Within the latter volumes, Shakespeare's name appears thrice and most of the information on Shakespeare is remarkably accurate, including the uniformed spelling of Shakespeare's name. The date and the place of publication of the *Passionate Pilgrim* (then incorrectly regarded as Shakespeare's work) is correct. Fulham notes that another book containing one hundred and fifty-four sonnets, together with *The Lover's Complaint* was issued in London in 1609, and these are the first mentions of either publication in the 17th century. Here are the brief biographical notes (slightly modernised) on Shakespeare contained within these volumes, with gaps filled in by Richard Davies.

> *William Shakespeare was born at Stratford-upon Avon in*
> *Warwickshire about 1563. From an Actor of Playes, he*
> *became a Composer. At 53, He dyed Apr. 23, 1616 probably*

at Stratford, for there he is buryed and hath a Monument.
Given to all unluckinesse in Stealing venison & Rabbits
particularly from Sr. Lucy who had him oft whipt &
sometimes Imprisoned & at last made Him fly his Native
Country to his great Advancement. But His revenge was so
great that he is his Justice Clodpate and calls him a great man
etc. and, in allusion to his name bore three lowses rampant
for his Arms.' Monument on which he lays a heavy curse upon
any one who shall remove his bones. He dyed a Papist.[79]

Shakespeare's curse upon anyone who removes his bones has very strong Catholic flavour. Catholics especially feared having their bones dug up and burnt to make way for more corpses as they believed their bodies should be in one piece for the resurrection. Not everyone, however, believed the stories of Fullman and Davies. Anthony Wood remarked that Davies 'looked red and jolly as if he had been at a fish dinner at Corpus Christie college and afterwards drinking as he had been.'[80] Wood implies that the Anglican priest may have been sloshed whilst jotting his contributions, but sober or drunk, another reason is that Davies may well have been influenced by the many connections Shakespeare had to the extraordinary Jesuit Robert Parsons. A priest who centuries after his death the novelist Evelyn Waugh described as 'the exemplar of the sinister Jesuit of popular imagination', while others called him 'the most reviled man in England'. Parsons story is a remarkable tale.[81]

In 1562, at the age of 16, Robert Parsons was sent to St Mary's Hall, Oxford. After completing his degree with distinction he became a fellow and a tutor at Balliol in 1568, where his extreme views often led to tense relations with his colleagues, even fellow Catholics such as the Roman Catholic priest and academic Christopher Bagshaw. On 13th February 1574, fiery Parsons clashed with Balliol college Master Adam Squire and he was left with no choice but to resign.[82] This may have been the catalyst which gave him the time and space to concentrate his efforts to become one of the leading players of the English mission of the Society of Jesus. Parsons travelled to Rome where he became a Jesuit priest at St Paul's on the 3rd July, 1575. Parsons then was responsible for organising the Roman Catholic resistance to the Queen Elizabeth's protestant regime and regularly consorted with Italy and Spain fully in favour of armed intervention. The influential priest was also alleged to have been involved in many plots against the Queen's life. A prolific pamphleteer with a strong belief in the power of propaganda, Parsons once reported to his Roman General, Claudio Aquaviva 'for there is nothing which helps and has helped and will protect in the future and spread our cause so much as the printing of Catholic books, whether of controversy or of devotion.'[83]

There is a very interesting link between Parsons and Shakespeare that has caused much speculation, and that is the latter's depiction of the rogue Sir John Falstaff in Henry IV. When Shakespeare first produced Henry IV Sir John Falstaff was originally named after the 15th century protestant Martyr, Sir John Oldcastle. The real Sir John Oldcastle, like Falstaff, was a close friend of King Henry V. King Henry tried his upmost to stick by the knight through numerous accusations of Lollard heresy to the crown. When Oldcastle became head of the Lollards' open rebellion, the King had no choice but to condemn his former friend and turn his back on their friendship, much like Henry V eventually turned against Falstaff in the play, but for completely different reasons. Nearly five years of cat and mouse hunting for Oldcastle led eventually to the discovery of Sir John's hiding place in the bleak Black Mountains of Wales, in November 1417. Oldcastle was brought to London by horse and cart and hung from the gallows the next month. As he choked, swaying in the fields of St Giles on this cold mid-December day, he was then set fire to 'gallows and all', claimed the witnesses.[84] Oldcastle was a deeply religious Protestant who believed in the writings of John Wyclyff[85] (as all Lollards did) that the church should be a poor establishment, not a grand and rich institution like the Catholic church had become. Essentially he was a Puritan who wouldn't touch a drop of ale and like other Puritans, not in favour of the theatre in which they viewed actors as liars (pretending to be something they were not) and didn't care for men dressed as women. I imagine they did not take too kindly to being mocked on stage, which happened often in the mischievous world of theatre. One needs to look no further than Malvolio in *Twelfth Night* to witness a teased and harassed Puritan. It was the straight laced Puritans under Oliver Cromwell who succeeded in closing the theatres down after the Civil War. Falstaff was everything the Puritan detested and in Henry IV part II, when Falstaff and Justice Shallow reminisce upon their youth, Falstaff states that 'we have heard the chimes at midnight' which means that they were up to no good as only the nefarious would be out that late at night! The gluttonous, hard drinking, skirt chasing vagabond stood for everything the Puritans would love to legislate against. Howls of protest came from the proud descendants of Sir John Oldcastle, furious over the gross depiction, and the name had to be altered. Thus Sir John Oldcastle became Sir John Falstaff, which some believe to be a pun on the name Shake-speare. Shakespeare would have had great difficulty entertaining the Elizabethan court if he did not comply with the complainant's wishes; one descendant, William Brooke, was the Lord Chamberlain, directly responsible for the Royal Court entertainments.[86]

A clever reference on the name of the martyr did escape the master of the revel's stern censorship; in the first scene Prince Hal affectionately calls Falstaff 'My old lad of the castle.' In 1604, Robert Parsons, utilizing Shakespeare's play as a platform for politics, made the following comments about 'Wycliffian' Oldcastle as being 'a ruffian knight as all England knoweth, commonly brought in by comedians on their stages'. Robert Parsons and Shakespeare are also linked together in a complaint against the pair over the Oldcastle depiction by the protestant writer John Speed in his 1611 edition of 'The theatre of the Empire of Great Britain'. Speed accused 'the Papist and his poet' that they were 'of like conscience for lies, the one ever faining and the other ever falsifying the truth'.[87] 51 years later the complaints regarding the Oldcastle depiction still manifested. In his patriotic tome 'Worthiness of England' Thomas Fuller bemoans that

> the stage hath been overbold with his memory, making him
> a thrasonical puff and emblem of mock valour. True it is, Sir
> John Oldcastle did first bear the brunt of the one, being made
> the make-sport in all plays for a coward. it is easily known
> out of what purse this black penny came: the papists railing
> on him for a heretic, and therefore must also be a coward,
> though indeed he was a man of arms, every inch of him, and
> as valiant as any in his age. Now I am glad that Sir John
> Oldcastle is put out, so I am sorry that Sir John Falstaff is put

> *in, to relieve his memory in this base service, to be the anvil*
> *of every dull wit to strike upon. nor is our comedian excusable*
> *by some alteration of his name, writing Sir John Falstafe (and*
> *making him the property of pleasure for King Henry the fifth*
> *to abuse) seeing the vicinity of sounds intrench on the memory*
> *of that worthy knight, and a few do heed the inconsiderable*
> *difference in spelling of their name.* [88]

Shakespeare certainly ruffled feathers with his characterisation of the puritanical Oldcastle and gave The head of the Jesuit movement ammunition for his propaganda.[89] Many scholars over the years have even stated that some of Shakespeare's works were directly influenced by Robert Parsons popular tome, *The Christian Directory*. The former Balliol man made an impression on many playwrights with this influential book; admirers included the often acerbic duo, Thomas Nashe and Robert Green. Father Peter Milward, who has written some meticulously researched books on Shakespeare's links with the Catholic faith, has provided a surprising example of a paragraph from Parsons' book that evokes strong parallels with *Hamlet's* famous 'to be or not to be' soliloquy.

> *Now, what puissance and valew of mynd think yow might*
> *suffice?*
> *noblenesse or courage wer nedefull? What strong and steadfast*
> *constancie do yow judge requisite to make men hable to beare*
> *and endure those vexations which before I have reported?*
> *Those contumelies (I mean) and those despites?*
> *(Parsons Epistle 158)*[90]

Even if mere coincidence, there is startling textual similarity, in both tone and language. If Shakespeare was a crypto-Catholic as many suspect, it's highly likely he read Parsons' influential works. Another connection between the poet and the Papist is that Parsons was a friend of the beheaded Edward Arden, which makes him inextricably linked as a family friend on Shakespeare's mother's side. A spiritual testament of faith was alleged to have been discovered in the rafters of John Shakespeare's house by workmen in 1757, confirming John Shakespeare's Catholic beliefs. The testament of faith was distributed by Edmund Campion[91] and Robert Parsons who led the Jesuit mission to England in 1580, an attempt to bolster the faith of the generally pious leaning Midlanders, which ultimately resulted in the capture and execution of the canonised Edmund Campion.

Unfortunately, Shakespeare's father's spiritual testament of faith has since disappeared, if it ever existed. Many scholars argue that John Shakespeare was clearly not a Catholic, remarking that he would not have joined in with the whitewashing of Catholic imagery that took place in the local churches, by order of government. John Shakespeare was a local dignitary and did not volunteer to erase memories of the old religion, but was obliged to. It was also not uncommon for people to claim to be a church-going Protestant and then call for a priest to attend their death bed. Charles II being a high profile example.

So we can connect the poet and the Oxford-educated Papist through literature, family connections high profile complaints and perhaps religion too. Though they may have crossed paths, Parsons was unlikely to have been in Oxford during Shakespeare's visits, though an inn built behind the college Parsons was forced to resign from, may unlock a few more doors to Shakespeare's faith.

14. A Famous Plot To Kill The King

If the front walls of Balliol had seen the horrific burning of Protestant bishops in 1555, and the walls inside privy to the whispers of Catholic assassins in the late 1580s, then the back walls were to witness the seedlings of a most famous plot to murder a monarch, the Gunpowder plot. Saint Catherine has always been associated with Balliol College, its dedication to the saint going back to its foundation. The Inn which operated from the 16th to the 18th century behind the college (now by the present college back gate) was called the Catherine Wheel Inn. This public house was a meeting point for Catholics, often used as a venue for secret mass and it was frequently raided by spymasters looking for recusants.

In July 5th 1589, two Catholic priests, Richard Yaxley and George Nichols and two layman, Thomas Belson and Humphey Pritchard, were executed after being arrested a fortnight earlier for celebrating mass at the Catherine Wheel. Nichols was Oxford born and bred, a Brasenose College man and Yaxley a Lincolnshire man. Yaxley and Nichols were hung, drawn and quartered in London, after suffering horrific torture in London, which involved being hung by their wrists for fifteen hours, following which they were returned to Oxford and dragged to the Oxford castle gallows by a horse-drawn hurdle. Their companions, Oriel college graduate Belson and Catherine Wheel Inn bar man, Welsh-born Prichard, were hung later the same day; their punishment for harbouring the priests. The decapitated heads of the four unfortunates were then set up on the castle gates, and their bodies scattered around the four town gates. Legend has it that Nichols' right arm swivelled round, pointing at the cursed city. The harshest of punishments served its purpose for the Protestant government as the crime of celebrating mass was not recorded for well over two decades.[92] The Catherine Wheel, surprisingly, didn't cease to be a hub for dangerous activity.

Guy Fawkes is the infamous name associated with the gunpowder plot. However, he was the muscle, a strong Lancashire man with vast military experience. Robert Catesby was the driving force and mastermind behind the plot and responsible for recruiting the conspirators. The Catholics were bitterly disappointed with King James, as they had at first held a glimmer of optimism when the King was crowned, after decades of brutal persecution during Queen Elizabeth's reign. Catesby was a dashing figure who came from a distinguished family and he was a descendant of Richard II's councillor Catesby, immortalised as 'The cat' by Shakespeare in the play *Richard II*. '*The Cat, the Rat and Lovel our Dog Doe rule all England under a Hog.*'[93] Catesby's family had close connections to Oxford; his father William once resided in Gloucester Hall (Worcester College) with his heavily pregnant wife. When she gave birth to Robert's sibling, the baby was given a Catholic baptism though the parish fees were paid to the distinctly Protestant parish of St Thomas, another curious indication of the schizoid religious state of the times.[94]

Gloucester hall was also the College Robert Catesby studied, though left the Catholic leaning establishment without a degree.

Robert Catesby had decided it was once again time for revolution, having already played a small part with Lord Southampton in the Earl of Essex's disastrous attempt to overthrow Queen Elizabeth. He had already recruited six co-conspirators before he had arranged a meeting with two others, Robert Wintour and John Grant at the Catherine Wheel Inn, mid-February 1605. On this late winters day at the Oxford inn, Catesby explained the ambitious plan to Grant and Wintour who then swore an oath and the plot to blow up parliament and change history was now in full swing. Wintour at first was not interested in taking part but was persuaded to follow the lead of his younger brother who was already deeply involved.[95]

Gunpowder plotters at the Catherine Wheel inn, Oxford by Danny Connor

Robert Wintour's heart was never really in it though and it is likely the persuasion took the form of peer pressure. Perhaps he just thought the plan wouldn't work and as history shows us it didn't. Fawkes, the gnarled army veteran, was apparently caught just before lighting the dynamite wick and the rest of the plotters were then hounded throughout the country and if not killed during raids then hung, drawn and quartered after their show trials.[96]

After the Southampton plot against Queen Elizabeth, Shakespeare and his players were scrutinised by the privy council for agreeing to perform *Richard II* complete with the banned deposition scene. On the eve of thev ill-fated Essex rebellion, Southampton had paid for a performance with the controversial scene included, the scene which suggested tyrannical monarchs could be removed by the people. Once again, in the aftermath of a regicidal plot, Shakespeare would have good cause for concern. Shakespeare was actually related to Robert Catesby through marriage to a cousin on his mother's side. On top of this, the plotter's father John Catesby was said to be friends with Shakespeare's father who on many occasions had been fined for being a recusant, though its often cited his absence was probably due to avoiding debtors.

With clear connections between the Shakespeares and the Catesbys, it is probably not a great surprise to discover that in the aftermath of the plot's discovery, William Shakespeare's oldest, Susannah became listed as a regular recusant, a dangerous time to draw attention to oneself for not attending church.[97] We cannot be sure how the playwright felt about these dramatic events. Could he have been privy to inside knowledge of the plot partially constructed by his distant relative at the Oxford inn and further developed in his favourite London watering hole, The Mermaid, a notorious stomping ground for turncoats. It is likely Shakespeare was a nervous man during the brutal executions of his fellow Midlanders and that whilst London crowds cheered the very public mutilation of Catesby and friends, astute Shakespeare busied himself with a play fit for the king's tastes, *Macbeth*.

I have always found it ironic that oaths were sworn to kill the king a mere two-minute walk from the building which sealed King James' legacy, the Bodleian library. The plot was also conceived just a few months after the King James bible project went into motion in 1604. The Bodleian library, positioned on Broad street, was built by the church primarily as a work station to translate for The King James authorised Bible, the most important tome of the English language ever produced, the Shakespeare folio a close second!

15. The King James Bible

The King James authorised version of the bible which was a revision of William Tyndale's translation, took the efforts of 47 educated clergy men. The grand work of vast research was carried out over four years in both Oxford and Cambridge with the final editing taking place in Westminster court, London.[98] King James, by far the most cultured monarch to sit upon the English throne, is a complex figure of contradictions. The Whig historian Macaulay summed up these contradictions with an interesting quote describing the monarch as 'made up of two men – a witty well-read scholar who wrote, disputed and harangued, and a nervous, drivelling idiot who acted.'[99] The King had a penchant for young attractive men whom he promoted to positions of great power, much to the chagrin of those who felt more deserving for such honours. Literature was another of the King's loves and he was exceptionally well read, assiduously promoting the Bible which carried his name, even if the Bible was produced partially to appease the Puritans. Shakespeare may not have shared the King's religious ideologies but he would have recognised the potential benefits of appeasing the King by eventually writing *Macbeth*.

Before delving into a fascinating Oxford connection between King James and Shakespeare's construction of *Macbeth*, I will look at the rather delightful myth of Shakespeare's involvement in writing sections of the King James Bible. [100]

Shakespeare and Ben Jonson are relaxing in Shakespeare's Stratford garden when suddenly a message for help arrives from the King James Bible translator, Miles Smith. Smith requires assistance translating a section of the book of Isaiah. Challenge accepted, Shakespeare and the great classicist Jonson study older translations of the work and produce a much improved piece which they send onward to Smith. Knowing that no-one would ever discover their collaborative involvement in the King James Bible, Ben Jonson asks 'Who will know we had part in it?' to which Shakespeare replies 'God, maybe if he ever lay ear to earth.' This conversation never took place and actually comes from Rudyard Kipling's charming tale *Proofs of holy writ*.[101] Kipling may have playfully pondered on the possibility that playwrights worked on the Bible whilst composing his short story, but for others the subject of Shakespeare's involvement in the Holy Book is one of serious debate.

Great minds, Shakespeare and the king discuss the bible at the Bodleian by Alex Singleton

In 1976 the Bishop Mark Hudson wrote to The Times regarding an amazing discovery that he had made. Clues actually left by Shakespeare indicated his involvement in work on the King James Bible. Hudson stated that 'if you look up Psalm 46 in the Authorized Version of the Bible and count 46 words from the beginning of the psalm, you will find that you have arrived at the word 'shake'. Now, discounting the word 'Selah', count 46 words from the end of the psalm and the word revealed is 'spear'. This astonishing cryptogram is virtually unknown. Psalm 46, 46th word from the beginning, 46th word from the end 'Shakespeare'. To cement the bishop's theory (probably to himself) is that Shakespeare was also 46 years old when he wrote psalm 46 in 1610. Investigating anachronisms and cryptic coding has been a popular game, especially since the coded works of Francis Bacon, himself a grand master of the complex art. The problem many scholars have with the bishop's theory is that a word has to be omitted for it to work, otherwise Shake is actually 47 words in and the Bishop admits this himself. If one searches long enough to find cryptic messages in books and plays, then codes can be discovered that don't really exist, as the Reverend did by conveniently removing a word to make his cryptic 'discovery' fit. I think an investigation should be conducted into the negligence of the Bishop's parishioners in 1976 as he clearly must have had too much time on his hands to be discovering such remarkable coincidences.

Even with the charming Kipling story and the shaky evidence from the code-breaking Bishop, it does seem rather fanciful. Nevertheless, it is an interesting footnote in the many legends surrounding Shakespeare's life. But the fanciful became more compelling when I read a quote on the Shakespeare authorship debate by Malcolm X in his 1965 biography, specifically a mistake made by the activist.

'I was intrigued by Shakespearian dilemma - not being able to prove Shakespeare's real identity. Some say he might have been Francis Bacon, but what if he was in fact king James himself?'

The King James translation of the Bible is considered the greatest piece of literature in English. It uses King's English perfectly, much like Shakespeare. They say that James got most famous poets of the time (early 17th century) to translate for the Bible. If Shakespeare existed, he was at the time the top poet around. But Shakespeare is nowhere to be connected with the Bible. If he existed why didn't James use him? And if he did, why is it one of the world's best kept secrets? I know that many say that Francis Bacon was Shakespeare. If that's true, what motive did Bacon have for keeping it a secret? What would Bacon have had to lose? Bacon, in fact, would have everything to gain. King James was brilliant, the greatest king who ever sat on English throne. He might have used 'nom de plume' Shakespeare because at the time it was improper for royalty to be artistic or theatrical. It was he who poetically 'fixed' the Bible as he had the intellectual capacity. '' Malcolm X[102]

I must point out that I will not waste energy on the authorship debate as I am a firm believer that Shakespeare wrote the plays his name is attached to. Due to great technological advances in linguistic forensics most scholars admit that he may have collaborated more than we would have imagined but nevertheless I believe Shakespeare to have been the main architect of the works attributed to him. The mistake Malcolm X makes in his statement that I find interesting, is not the assumption that the translators were all poets – in that sense he is right – it is that Malcolm X didn't acknowledge that all of the 47 known translators had to be officially ordained men of the church, to confirm the Bible's authenticity as a holy tome. All 47 were members of the Church of England in some context and it is not commonly thought that 'James got most top poets around', which makes one wonder that if Shakespeare and Jonson had helped with a small part of the translations of the most prolific book printed in the English language, their names would have to be missing from the official translations records as neither were men of the cloth. Which is to say that any poet's involvement is certainly not implausible but also not recordable, and therefore never provable. Though it is highly likely that Shakespeare and his peers, Jonson, Spencer and the other giants from this golden age of literature, would have greatly influenced the poetic language of the Bible, with its rich sonorous style that today we may take for granted.

Incidentally on the subject of Malcolm X, though he was clearly sceptical that Shakespeare wrote the plays, that did not stop him on a 1965 visit to Oxford's debating chamber from reciting excerpts from *Hamlet's* 'to be or not to be' speech to exemplify 'intelligently directed extremism', the gist being that nothing could be achieved by suffering the slings and arrows of outrageous fortunes.[103] There is an Oxford Myth that Shakespeare visited the Bodleian library, but if he did he most likely only saw it from the outside as the Library is infamous for its strict policies. Even King Charles I was forbidden from removing a book from the library. Though Shakespeare was a King's man and that may have held some sway. If he did achieve access it was highly unlikely he would have discovered any plays to peruse. We can ascertain the Bodleian founder's views on including plays within the library's early collections, when he wrote 'haply some plays may be worthy the keeping, but hardly one in forty'.

Having the privilege of being a King's man meant Shakespeare had a duty to please his Patron and an incident concerning King James' 1605 Oxford visit could certainly have helped Shakespeare shape an important part of his great tribute to the Scottish King, the Scottish play *Macbeth*.

16. Three Witches At The Gates Of St John's

In 1605, a man named Matthew Gwynn who was a tutor at St John's College, Oxford was often in charge of organising plays and events for special occasions. Thirteen years earlier he had devised plays at Christ Church and organised debates on moral philosophy for the pleasure of Queen Elizabeth on her 1592 Oxford visit. He was a man with many remarkable interweaving yet separate links to Shakespeare and John Davenant.

Gwynn's brother Roger became the fourth and final husband to an Anglo-Flemish lady called Susan who was at one stage married to John Davenant's cousin Thomas Gore, her first husband. Susan was also perceived to be the mother of King's man actor and Shakespeare friend, Nicholas Tooley. [104]When the recently crowned King James visited the University of Oxford on 29th August, Matthew Gwynn was once again head of the festivities. At Christchurch the players of St John's performed a play written by Gwynn, a comedy entitled *Vertumnus Sive Annus Recurrens*. The play started at 9pm, finished at 1am and King James may have been exhausted, drunk, bored or perhaps all three; he dozed off in the great hall before the play's finale. Earlier in the day Gwynn had organised a pageant which would have appealed to the king on many levels, notably with regards to his intense interest in witchcraft.

As the King entered Oxford he was greeted by three young students, dressed in the female attire of sibyls. The three appeared from an arbour of ivy, they took turns to hail him King of Scotland, King of England and King of Ireland. The King was reminded that the Thane Banquo had been foretold by three prophesying sisters that though he would never be King, his descendants would one day rule an empire. As the monarch claimed descent from Banquo, the three cross-dressed sisters were confirming the prophecy. The speeches were recited in Latin and afterwards in English, following which the King applauded the performance. This display of mock supernatural entertainment, outside the grand St John's college, on a fine summer morning, would have pleased the King heartily, as any confirmation of his right to the throne would have during the early and perhaps insecure days of his reign. The King was famed for dishing out plenty of knighthoods as soon as he came to power. This may have upset the established gentry but certainly made him more friends than enemies, and friendships were important to a king viewed as foreign to many Englanders.

The supernatural aspect of the boy actor's greetings, especially the prophecies, would have stirred something within the King, who was riddled with anxieties over ghosts and spirits. When the King wrote his eighty-page book on witchcraft, *Daemonologie*, he stated that practitioners of black magic would give deceptive and double-meaning prophecies. The King had a long-term obsession with the supernatural and on the evening prior to his mother's execution, a very young James apparently told Lord Harrington that he had witnessed an apparition of 'a bloody head dancing in the air'. In 1590 a storm threatened to destroy a ship that the King and his newlywed bride were sailing on from Copenhagen to Scotland. The tempest was blamed on witchcraft and near a hundred suspected witches were tortured till they confessed. It wasn't only ghosts that scared the monarch, he was also known to be petrified of meeting a violent death and wore seven layers of clothing to protect himself from the daggers of would be assassins.

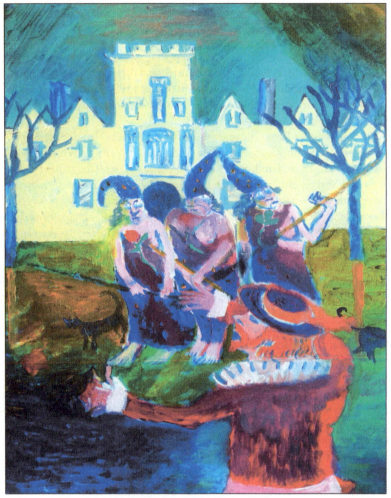

The weird sisters at St Johns by Alex Singleton

There is a romantic notion that the three sibyls' appearance inspired Shakespeare to include the prophesying sisters in *Macbeth*. The notion is that Shakespeare, over a glass of wine, perhaps at the Crown Inn, heard of the big topical news regarding the King's visit, probably from his friend, the innkeeper John Davenant[105], who attended the King's royal procession through Oxford, as a local Council official. Davenant would have witnessed the sight of the three prophesying sisters, mentioned the event to Shakespeare who would then incorporate the memorable prophecies into his grand tribute to the King, *Macbeth*. The supervisor of the Royal festivities, Matthew Gwynn, may well have been at the Crown inn to meet with Shakespeare, given his connections to Davenant via Susan Gwynn, as well as his obvious informed interest in plays. [106]Shakespeare's portrayal of the three sisters as witch-like hags would also have appealed to the King's fascination with the paranormal. There was also some speculation that Macbeth was modelled on Robert Catesby. King James was heartbroken when he discovered Catesby had been central to the plot against him as the King regarded him as an ally, in the same way King Duncan regarded Macbeth, ultimately his nemesis. King James saw himself as a cultured intellectual, a worldly figure, not that dissimilar to Shakespeare's portrayal of King Duncan!

17. The Call For Oxford Men

On November 22nd, 2011, I attended a marvellous talk at the old Bodleian library given by Dr Emma Smith, an expert in the field of Shakespearian studies. There are dozens of her brilliant podcasts on all manner of Shakespeare related topics, available on the Bodleian's website. This talk centred on the return to the Bodleian library of a book which had been missing for 250 years and the mission which ensued to ensure it would never leave the library again.

On Monday 23rd January, 1905, Magdalen College undergraduate, Gladwyn Turbutt, strolled into the Bodleian to seek advice on the restoration of a Shakespeare book which had been resting in his father's Derbyshire library. When he handed over the book Falconer Madan, the sub Librarian, Madan was shocked. To his amazement, this was a 1623 first folio, that had been given to the Bodleian in 1624 under an agreement with the stationer's guild that a copy of every book published would be presented to the Bodleian. It had been missing for just over 250 years, probably sold off as a job lot of surplus, redundant books when the 'improved' third folio was published in 1664. We may look back in disbelief that the famous Bodleian could part with a first folio, but it was during a period in which Shakespeare's popularity had waned and the University was still reeling from the heavy financial blows of the English Civil War. It could also be the case that the Bodleian's first folio had quite simply been stolen. Upon seeing the smooth plain brown cover, Madan immediately summoned a colleague with an expertise in early binding to inspect the book and he confirmed what Madan had suspected. They compared four other books which had been sent to the Oxford binder, William Wildgoose, in 1624. The markings on the back of the books, with diagonal hatchings, all matched the markings of this first folio. To spread the joy of this remarkable find, Madan had two hundred folio-sized pamphlets privately printed and paid for by subscription, a souvenir of the miraculous discovery, offering a detailed description of the folio and a narrative regarding its manifestation.

Madan took the financial risks himself and arranged for the costs of the pamphlet, five shillings each, to be sent to his college address of Brasenose rather than the Bodleian, a move executed because he had initially kept the arrival of the folio a secret from his superior, Edward Nicolson. The sub-librarian was often at loggerheads ideologically with the head librarian, former Trinity man, Nicholson, they were very much contrasting librarians. Madan was a traditionalist, a scholarly respected veteran of twenty year's service to the Bodleian. He was now in his mid-fifties, an expert in the field of manuscript cataloguing and a founder member of the Bibliography society. On the other hand, ambitious Nicholson was a progressive archivist. In his undergraduate days he was uninterested in his studies, his passions were to be the Oxford Union librarian and he was a modernizer inspired by the American library models of the time. One thing that the two conflicting personalities could agree upon was the great importance in procuring the permanent return of the folio to what they believed as its rightful home. They both approached Gladwyn Turbutt's father separately with ideas to purchase the folio via subscription. Unfortunately, Madan's trumpet-blowing pamphleteering of the folio reappearance had reached the ear of a competitor for its ownership, an extremely wealthy competitor.

The London based booksellers Sotherans, had forwarded as an offer to the Turbutt family the enormous figure of £3,000 from 'an important foreign customer'. This was an astonishing, competition-quashing figure. To put the large offer into context, the most anyone had ever paid for a well-conditioned Shakespeare folio of any edition, was £800. The highest amount the Bodleian had ever spent on a book was £200. Wealthy land owner, Turbutt senior had intended for the book to remain with the family as an heirloom, but the great agricultural depression of the 19th century, the exceptionally high death duty tax rates, and the astonishingly high financial offer were all incentives to part with the folio. At this time of economic uncertainty, there was a pattern developing among struggling English gentry, selling off their antiques and valuable art to foreign interested parties, predominantly Americans. This notion was not lost on the savvy art dealers of the time, some of whom made millions from the European aristocrats.[107] British born Baron, Joseph Duveen was one of the most successful art dealers of this period. His simple business model can be summed up in his own words, 'Europe has a great deal of art, and America has a great deal of money.'[108]

Nicholson was desperate to have the folio back at the Bodleian and decided to try to match the offer from the mysterious party by asking Oxford's rich alumni to provide donations for its purchase. The head of the library sent a prospectus to all of the heads of house, asking who were the colleges' richest men and then proceeded to contact those on his wealthy list. Time was running out, Turbutt senior gave the Bodleian a deadline of 31st March to match the offer but by 11th March only £1,300 had been raised. It was time for a desperate measure; Nicholson took to writing a call out for Oxford men in The Times. He warned 'It is practically certain that this offer comes from the United states and the danger is real that this would be lost forever, not only to us but to Shakespeare's fatherland, that after two and a half centuries we should have the extraordinary chance of recovering this volume, and should lose it because a single American can spend more money than all Oxford sons or friends that have been helping us is a bitter prospect.' The Times chipped in with 'In another country the government would help in such a case, Oxford and the Bodleian stand in proud isolation asking nothing from the state'. The impassioned, patriotic wording stirred Oxford men into action and the funds were raised almost immediately. Turbutt senior was moved by this call to arms and decided to knock £200 off the price. The Times followed the story with the great headline 'Shakespeare is saved'. An elated Nicholson couldn't wait for the library to receive the first folio. He was unaware it had been on the library premises since Gladwyn Turbutt had walked in with it.

The sub-librarian Madan was delighted but compiled a list of Oxford men who declined to donate, the list of shame included the Regis professor of English literature, the University Chancellor, the vice Chancellor and the keeper of the Ashmolean museum. The inspired appeal and the Oxford men who answered the call, ensured that the first folio stayed in Shakespeare's fatherland and out of the clutches of the American multimillionaires, namely in this case, as it transpired, Henry Clay Folger, who by 1906, had attained twenty-six first folios in his laboratory (as he called his world famous library) and would go on to own another fifty; more than a third of the world's known first folios in existence. [109]

What came of the unsung hero, young Gladwyn Turbutt, the Magdalen college undergraduate who unknowingly returned the folio to its original home? He moved back to his home of Derbyshire, where he ploughed on with his career as an architect, with a passion for early Norman architecture. He was also a justice of the peace and a commissioner for the local boy scouts.

When the Great War began in 1914, Lieutenant Gladwyn Maurice Revell Turbutt was sent with the Oxfordshire and Buckinghamshire light infantry, into the bloody hell hole of Ypres, Belgium. The first battle of Ypres took place October 21st, 1914. Two days into the battle Turbutt was dead. He was only 30 years old. There is a legend that he told his men stories of victories of Henry V in Agincourt before they themselves went into combat. Volume One of a book called The Bond of Sacrifice, which recorded the deaths of all British soldiers who fell in the Great War, was published in 1917. Within the pages of this catalogue of death, there is a tribute to Gladwyn Turbutt, which confirms something that we already know, 'a love for all that was ancient and beautiful marked his undergraduate days'.[110]

18. Shakespeares Patron, Mr W. H.

The main square of the old Bodleian library, the Old Schools Quad, is a mightily impressive sight. The quad is perfectly square for when Oxford clergy researched ancient tomes to complete translations for the King James authorised Bible, they read that the old temple of Solomon in Jerusalem was perfectly square and so designed the quad with this in mind to symbolise the perfection of divine knowledge. On each corner of the quad, emblazoned above each door, are the subjects that were taught centuries ago, in Latin off course. The entrance to the Divinity school occupies the west side of the square. When Charles I set up camp in Oxford during the Civil War, Oxford became the royal capital of England, the Divinity school acted as King Charles' House of Commons. Facing the Divinity school is the imposing tower of the five orders. Perched near the top of the tower is a statue of Charles' father, King James, in all his splendid glory, arms outstretched, holding two books; one book an obscure work of his own, the second the famed work he commissioned, The King James authorised version of the Bible.

If you were to enter the Divinity school now, you would be faced with a striking bronze statue of an Earl suggested by many to have been Shakespeare's muse for the first 126 sonnets, a man criminally overlooked in the history of 17th century arts, William Herbert, the 4th Earl of Pembroke, a man who had in his life 'prosecuted. . . with so much favour'. Published by Thomas Thorpe, in 1609 (at the height of Shakespeare's fame) the sonnets are a collection of 154 poems written by Shakespeare and contain some of the most insightful poetry regarding love and passion ever written in the English language. The publication ends with A Lover's Complaint– a poem of 47 line stanzas.

It is interesting to note that though we now hold the sonnets in such high regard, the Thorpe publication was not a great success and, unlike his popular plays, never reprinted during Shakespeare's lifetime; it is probable that the fashion for such poetry had dwindled. For monetary reasons Shakespeare may well have been holding back the publication of his sonnets until the theatres were inevitably closed down by plague, by which stage they may well have been out of vogue. The first seventeen sonnets urge a young man to marry so his beauty will be immortalized for the next generation. Other Sonnets are preoccupied with the passage of time and dwell upon death, mortality, and the poet's passion for the 'fair youth' as well as his jealousy raging from the young subject's preference for a rival poet. Complex feelings are expressed towards the speaker's mistress, the enigmatic dark lady.

We can deduce that the sonnets were written at least a decade before Thorpe's publication, as poems 138 and 144 were published in 1599 by the piratical William Jaggard in his small unauthorised hodgepodge compendium of plays and poems *The Passionate Pilgrim*. We know from Frances Mere's curious commonplace book *Palladis Tamia* that by 1598 Shakespeare was noted for his sonnets. Mere's *Palladis* is a vitally important source of information and critique on Tudor poets and playwrights as it is within this book that Shakespeare is first mentioned as a sonneteer. 'The sweete wittie soul of Ovid lives in mellifluous & honey-tongued Shakespeare, witness his Venus and Adonis, his Lucrece, his sugared sonnets among his private friends'. High praise indeed from the Oxbridge poet chronicler who also references the brutal demise of Marlowe.[111] For centuries generations have scrutinised, marvelled, psychoanalysed and fallen in love with these mysterious sugared sonnets. Vexingly mysterious for many reasons, who was the fair youth? And what is the identity of the dark lady? Who is the rival poet whose attraction for the youth makes the speaker jealous? A scandal is brought to light which the speaker has endured, was there any truth to it?

It is not uncommon to assume the perplexing sonnets are autobiographical and as a result contemporary biographers and critics scour writings to search for clues. This leads to the problem of Presentism, the tendency to view life from centuries past though modern eyes, and assume the people of the past perceived the world as we do, interpreting past events with an uncritical adherence to modern day attitude. Shakespeare may well have had no emotional attachment to the poems whatsoever, although I feel that the intense impassioned nature of the poetry makes that cynical notion unlikely. The clincher for myself is that at least some sections of the poems were personal and therefore were not originally intended for public consumption, to be circulated only to the literati, or as Meres mentioned 'amongst his private friends' unlike the plays enjoyed by the commoners. In the rather sordid Sonnet 135, Shakespeare even references his own name in a series of canny puns on the word Will, a sonnet I shall discuss in more detail later in this section. If the identities of the sonnets' subjects were not already frustratingly mysterious then to add further intrigue there is the bizarre dedication on the preface of the booklet

> *TO. THE. ONLIE. BEGETTER. OF.*
> *THESE. INSUING. SONNETS.*
> *Mr. W. H. ALL. HAPPINESSE.*
> *AND. THAT. ETERNITIE.*
> *PROMISED.*

BY.
OUR. EVER-LIVING. POET.
WISHETH.
THE. WELL-WISHING.
ADVENTURER. IN.
SETTING.
FORTH.

T. T.

Besides the fact that no one really knows what 'onlie begetter 'means, we also have a dedication which has provoked intense speculation. The term Mister is not how a typical patron, a noble of high ranking would be addressed as it is far too informal, though perhaps this was partially to conceal the identity of the dedicatee, the informal tone does suggest an intimacy. Perhaps, as Katherine Duncan Jones suggests, Shakespeare was simply too preoccupied escaping plagues or attending to property matters (or both) to concern himself with the dedications,[112] and left them to the publishers to compose. Even with the advances of modern linguistic technology, the dating of the sonnets is rather sketchy though most scholars agree they were probably begun in the early 1590s and completed and perhaps tinkered with before the Thorpe publication of 1609. If you agree with the great Shakespeare scholar Stanley Wells that the sonnets were not written in the order that they are presented, then there is certainly more leeway for speculation as to the identity of MR W. H. In the surprisingly long list of candidates for the dedication, two clearly standout. If you switch the initials then Henry Wriothesley, 3rd earl of Southampton is a proposed favourite. Southampton was an androgynous man in his youth, pretty, powerful and intelligent. The playwright George Peele described him in 1595 as 'Gentle and debonair'. Shakespeare's two early saucy poems, *Venus and Adonis* and *The Rape of Lucrece* were certainly dedicated to Southampton, the wording of the second dedication was particularly strong 'The love I dedicate to your lordship is without end…what I have done is yours, what I have to do is yours, being part in all I have, devoted yours.' It was Southampton who urged Shakespeare, Burbage and co to revive Richard II on the eve of the disastrous Essex rebellion, a bold action which put Southampton in prison.

When King James was crowned, Southampton was back in court, though only as a bit player. Like most nobles he was opposed to James' favourite, George Villier, the Duke of Buckingham who had risen from complete obscurity primarily due to his talent for tickling the King's fancy.

I believe the dashing figure who greets thousands of visitors each year to the Bodleian library's Divinity school, is our Mr W. H., the dedicatee, if not necessarily also the muse, and it is certainly worth an in-depth look at the man who has left a somewhat forgotten legacy, to the arts and to the culture of Oxford University.

19. The Hamlet Of King Charles' Court

William Herbert, 3rd Earl of Pembroke, was the richest nobleman of his time and the most important patron and protector of the arts in the 17th century. A powerful courtier whose career spanned the reigns of Elizabeth, James I and Charles I, Pembroke's proudest achievement was attaining the role of Chancellor of Oxford University. To remark that young William Herbert was raised in a literary household would be an understatement. His Father, the 2nd Earl of Pembroke sponsored a group of players as early as 1575, Pembroke's men. Pembroke's acting troupe performed Thomas Kyd's early version of *Hamlet* and Taming of the Shrew, and Shakespeare was briefly associated with Pembroke's men from around 1592–1594.[113] It would be hardly surprising if Shakespeare met the young noble William through this association.

William Herbert's mother, Mary Sidney, was a highly educated, cultured intellectual and poet. She mastered French, Hebrew, Latin and Greek and was probably the greatest patron of the arts till her son took over that mantle. Eminent poets Edmund Spenser and Thomas Nashe would seek her out for guidance. Mary Sidney's brother Phillip Sidney, the revered soldier poet, is still regarded as one of England's greatest poets and his Arcadia is still regarded as a work of genius, his sister incidentally serving as an inspiration.[114]

As a child of eleven years of age, Pembroke's tutor boldly stated that 'he had no equal for learning among all the peers of England' and at the age of twelve, March 1593 he matriculated at New College, Oxford.[115] Pembroke didn't take a degree and left around 15, probably because his ailing father sought a potential marriage alliance for his young son. During this period his father introduced him to his Godmother, Queen Elizabeth. Pembroke's introduction to Elizabethan court was somewhat of a disaster which perpetually tarnished his reputation. The Queen was regarded as protector of her maids of honour but this did not stop fifteen-year-old Pembroke from impregnating one such maid, seventeen-year-old Mary Fitton. The queen was livid and young Pembroke was sent to the prison of the fleet, then holed up in Baynard's castle before he was eventually exiled to the family home in Wilton.[116] Pembroke's reputation took a hammering for centuries to come.

The grand Clarendon building next to the Old Schools quad (which housed the University press) was financed by the success of the Earl of Clarendon's immensely popular *History of the Rebellion and Civil Wars in England.* Clarendon's wildly successful book tarnishes Pembroke as 'Immoderately given up to women...to this he sacrificed himself, his precious time, and much of his fortune.' Clarendon was an ally to King James' favourite, the unpopular Buckingham, who was Pembroke's main political opponent, so perhaps we can take Clarendon's remarks with a pinch of salt. The 20th century drama expert J. Dover Wilson, who also believed Pembroke to be Mr W. H., also stuck the boot in, writing that Pembroke 'was given to the detestable practise of enjoying women out of mere curiosity'. Clarendon and Wilson were not alone in dishing out negative views. 19th century historian S. R. Gardiner remarked 'he passed easily from hot opposition to the tamest submission, with an intelligence greater than the power of will, he was the Hamlet of Charles' court'[117]

Like Southampton, Pembroke's luck changed for the better when King James was crowned and on 19th March 1604 when the King's first Parliament met, his first spokesman in the House of Commons was William Herbert.[118] At the Herbert family residence in Wilton, 2nd December the previous year, Pembroke supervised the first play King James ever saw in England. Pembroke's interest in the arts and his dancing prowess enabled him to become heavily involved with the Court Masques, much to his great delight. The Masques were extremely important occasions and served as diplomatic functions. They were the primary focus of court life and a vital cog in the wheels of foreign policy development. It would have been with great delight that Pembroke participated on 6th January 1605 with Ben Jonson's first joint effort with the pioneering set designer and stage manager Inigo Jones on Jonson's famous *Masque of Darkness*.[119]

In 1611 Pembroke was promoted to the Privy Council and four years later made Lord Chamberlain. It is not by chance that in 1615 the control of staging plays and the responsibilities for the production of the Masques was taken from the Privy Council and passed unto the Lord Chamberlain. Pembroke, in this role he would have relished, was also bequeathed the licensing of books. Former Lord Chamberlains such as Lord Cobham had been strict executers of censorship. Fortunately for the dramatists of the day, their new Lord Chamberlain was the greatest patron of the arts ever. His approach was far from rigid and allowed drama to flow freely.[120]

A minor poet himself, exceptionally wealthy and famed for his impassioned yet discerning patronage, the literati of the age looked to him for support. He, more than any other, surpassed their wildest dreams. Whatever his peers' thoughts on Pembroke's poetry, his position as their most sought after patron was beyond dispute. Apart from poem and play dedications, 80 per cent of all religious works were dedicated to him upon his appointment as Chancellor of Oxford.[121] Pembroke always regarded the chancellorship of Oxford University as his finest achievement and it was during his chancellorship at Oxford that he awarded his lifelong friend Ben Jonson an M. A. [122]

In modern times, during the summer months, theatre companies occasionally perform in the old school's quad in the Bodleian. in 2014 I watched a performance of *King Lear* by the Globe on tour. An impressive oak and thatch Elizabethan replica stage was positioned with William Herbert's effigy still facing the drama, still presiding over Shakespeare's works as he would have done centuries earlier.

20. To Thy Sweet Will

I find it fascinating comparing different commentaries on Shakespeare's sonnets. I have recently been perusing both Katherine Duncan Jones Arden' edition of *Shakespeare's Sonnets* and Don Patterson's Reading *Shakespeare's Sonnets*. They have very different but excellent approaches to dissecting the sonnets. Duncan Jones is quite scholarly and Patterson is very humorous. Sonnet 135 is centred on clever wordplay and sex, the wordplay on the name Will I alluded to earlier.

The word Will is mentioned 13 times and adopts different meanings throughout the sonnet. For example, in this poem, the word Will often refers to a sexual organ (male or female) the line 'whose will is large and Spacious' implies that sexual promiscuity has enlarged the female subject's vagina.[123] 'Will will fulfil' implies in a rather boastful manner that William will fulfil his partners sexual desire as well as his own. There is a line in Sonnet 135 which Patterson points out satisfies the Pembrokites, the supporters of Pembroke as Shakespeare's muse. 'Will to boot and will in overplus' [124]

This line infers that not only is the author, Will Shakespeare (to boot) in the mix but that there is also an additional Will (in overplus). This complements the theory of William (Will) Herbert being subtly named and suggested as embroiled in a steamy love triangle. To me It seems clear that the sonnets were written over a period of 16 years, with the majority finished within the first ten, often plague ravaged years. I agree with leading Shakespearian scholar Stanley Wells that the sonnets were not written in the order that they are presented. My feeling is that Shakespeare may have had both Southampton and Pembroke in mind as dedicatees at different times, dependent on who was the flavour of the time, or on whom was not in hot water with the authorities. The sharp business acumen of Shakespeare would not continue dedicating works to Southampton whilst he was wasting away in the tower, even if he was the original muse.

As mentioned earlier Southampton never again scaled the great heights of power he was accustomed to, even after his release following the King's accession. It was the younger noblemen William Herbert who was an all-powerful statesman with a well-informed interest in the arts during the Stuart era. The perfect patron for Shakespeare to switch allegiance to. And if the poems seemed old hat to the public they were perhaps more popular within the homosocial atmosphere of King James' court. It is plain to see the switches of poets' preferred patrons coinciding with the rises in power and fortunes of differing nobles. The fair youth Southampton was Shakespeare's early dedicatee before he was embroiled in plots against the Queen. Then when Southampton was old news it was William Herbert and his Brother Philip who were immortalised in the First folio dedication. 'To the most noble and incomparable pair of brethren'. And though Shakespeare was seven years dead when his collected works were published, his old savvy partners Heminges and Condell made sure to thank the Herbert's on the late Shakespeare's behalf for past favours to the playwright. 'Since your lordships have been pleased to think these trifles something, heretofore, and have prosecuted both them, and their author living, with so much favour'. [125]

Pembroke's favours to the legacy of Shakespeare's works continued well after his death. In 1619 he fought to protect the rights of the Players, attempting to prevent the plays of the King's men from being printed in the capital 'without some of their consents'. Alas, strongly worded letters to the Company of Printers and Stationers would achieve little in the frenzied publishing world of 17th century England.[126] If one stands near Pembroke's statue long enough during peak tourist season, you will inevitably hear tour guides point at the statue and gleefully inform the crowd that this Chancellor of the University had a sexual relationship with Shakespeare. If Pembroke was the fair youth who betrayed the poet by having an affair with the dark lady, it certainly wasn't whilst Chancellor of Oxford as you would be led to believe. Pembroke was appointed Chancellor in 1616 at the age of 36, hardly a fair youth, and this was also the year Shakespeare died!

It is interesting that Mary Fitton, the maid of honour who became Pembroke's mistress, has been put forward numerous times as a candidate for the tempting dark lady of the love triangle. Notably proposed by Thomas Tyler in the 1890 sonnets edition and Frank Harris in his strange biography, *Shakespeare the man* (1909), though this notion is usually dismissed by modern scholars, even those who believe Pembroke to be the fair youth. [127]

Although we will never know the true nature of the relationship between this nobleman and the poet. We do however know that Pembroke loved plays and loved players. In 1619 William Herbert struggled emotionally to sit through a performance of Pericles, as the revered actor, King's player and close friend to the Earl, Richard Burbage had recently passed. On this sad subject Pembroke wrote to Lord Doncaster 'the whole company were at play, which I, being tender hearted could not endure to see so soon after the loss of My old aquaintance Burbadg'.[128]

21. Pembroke's Legacy

As asserted earlier, Pembroke has had numerous detractors over the centuries and many who enjoy highlighting his faults rather than his vast achievements. 'Pembroke did labour as for his life all the reign of King James to be of the bedchamber and could never obtain it' sighed the Duke of Newcastle in doom and gloom fashion,[129] as though Lord Chamberlain and Chancellor of Oxford were not achievements. It is rather ironic that Pembroke's statue is positioned next to Clarendon House, a building funded by the success of Edward Hyde's *The History of the Rebellion*, the book which tarnished Pembroke's reputation, painting him as sex obsessed and willing to sacrifice all for a tumble in a haystack. Pembroke's effigy also has to put up with eternally being looked down upon by King James' statue.[130] Pembroke's legacy however, as the protector of the Arts is incalculable. His legacy to Oxford not only includes his prized chancellorship but also the founding of Pembroke College in 1624, the letters patent of which were signed by King James in order to found the college. And Pembroke College had a very famous student with an extremely important contribution to the critical analysis of Shakespeare's entire works.

22. Dr Samuel Johnson At Pembroke

The eccentric but brilliant lexicographer Samuel Johnson entered Pembroke College at the age of 19. He is considered by many to be one of the key influences on the English language. The college has retained two curious items that belonged to Dr Johnson. One is a massive tea cup which he drank copious amounts of tea from. The second, his rather large ice skates which he wore when skating along the frozen Thames that runs through Christ Church meadow. After completing the small task of writing his famous *A Dictionary of the English Language*, he then moved onto Shakespeare's works, providing a template for modern Shakespearian criticism, which was published 10th October 1765, seven years after the intended date of publication. This led to a rather humorous problem, as although a meticulous annotator he was an awful accountant and struggled to recall who had paid in advance for the works subscribed almost a decade earlier.[131]

He unfortunately had to leave Pembroke after 13 months having run out of funds. His old college did recognise his achievements and awarded him a master of the arts shortly after the publication of his famed dictionary. The academically gifted Johnson and his brilliant actor friend Garrick both in their own very different ways contributed greatly towards the increased awareness of Shakespeare in the 18th Century. Johnson's critical analyses far surpassing the achievements of previous editors and Garrick's epic theatrical contributions leading to a mass popularising of Shakespeare, changing the bard from a man into a God.

23. Another Portrait Of Mr W. H.

Ten years after leaving Magdalen College and failing to be elected for the Oxford student union, the flamboyant genius Oscar Wilde wrote a brilliant short story, *The portrait of Mr W. H.* Though the tale is very short at 40 pages, Wilde must have researched the sonnets and stories attached to them with the investigative doggedness of a detective, just like his protagonists. The story revolves around three men who at various stages drive themselves to the brink of despair and beyond with their obsessions to solve the puzzle – Who is Mr W. H, the sonnets' dedicatee? Without giving too much away for those who haven't read the tale, one of the obsessive's, student actor Cyril Graham, comes up with a theory that Mr W.H. could not have been of high birth.[132] Citing sonnet 25 in which Shakespeare contrasts himself with those who are 'great prince's favourites'

> *Let those who are in favour with their stars,*
> *Of public honour and proud titles boast,*
> *Whilst I, whom fortune of such triumph bars,*
> *Unlook'd for joy in that I honour most.*

Cyril remarks that Shakespeare congratulates himself on 'the mean state of him he so adored' within the last two lines of the same sonnet: 'then happy I, that love and am beloved, where I may not remove nor be removed'. Cyril Graham later argues his corner, quite convincingly that Mr W.H. was a young actor,[133] citing sonnet 38

> *How can my muse want subject to invent,*
> *While thou dost breathe, that pour'st into my verse*
> *Thine own sweet argument, too excellent*
> *For every vulgar paper to rehearse?*
> *O! give thy self the thanks, if aught in me*
> *Worthy perusal stand against thy sight;*
> *For who's so dumb that cannot write to thee,*
> *When thou thy self dost give invention light?*
> *Be thou the tenth Muse, ten times more in worth*
> *Than those old nine which rhymers invocate*
> *And he that calls on thee, let him bring forth*
> *Eternal numbers to outlive long date.*

Cyril proceeds to proclaim a boy actor by the name of Willie Hughes as Shakespeare's inspiration, but then drives himself to madness trying to prove it. Fortunately, I have not gone insane obsessing over the identity of Mr W.H. and have always been in the corner of the two Earls, Southampton and Pembroke. However, upon reading Wilde's book, I considered the possibility that Henry Willobie is a potential contender for the enigmatic Mr W.H., the Oxford student who allegedly wrote the controversial and popular novella, *Willobie his Avisa*. I am not convinced as Wilde's character Cyril Graham was, that Mr W.H. was not of high birth. Henry Willobie was clearly from noble stock, raised in Wiltshire, a mere 18 miles from Wilton House which housed the important Pembroke family. Willobie was certainly young enough to have been the fair youth, having written the novella at around 17 years of age, matriculating at Oxford around 15. In the book, the author Willobie describes himself as a new actor (like Cyril's candidate Willie Hughes) and W.S. is described as an old player, which is particularly tantalising if you apply Wilde's detective stratagem on the sonnets and conclude Mr W.H. was an actor. The young actor Henry Willobie even competing with Shakespeare for the passions of the virtuous Inn keeper's wife (possibly Jennet Davenant), bringing to mind the sonnets' love triangle.

There is also the point that the initials fit Mr W.H., though obviously the wrong way round. When Hadrian Dorrell wrote the epistle to the first reprint of *Wilobie his Avisa*, he implied that some of the suitors were based on real individuals when he states.

> *"especially the matter and manner of their talks and*
> *conferences, me thinks it a matter almost impossible that any*
> *man could invent all this without some ground or foundation*
> *to build on, This inforceth me to conjecture, that though the*
> *matter be handled poetically, yet there is something under*
> *these fained names and showes that hath bene done truly."*[134]

I recently came across a fascinating link,[135] that Shakespeare's close friend from the Midlands, Thomas Russell was married to the sister of a woman named Eleanor Bampfield, Eleanor married Henry Willobie's older brother William Willobie, which implies the not unrealistic notion that Henry Willobie and the older player, Shakespeare, knew one another. As I will discuss in more detail later, Thomas Russell's stepson Leonard Digges, contributed poetry in the tributary preface of the first folio.

Is Henry Willobie our Mr W.H., the ill-fated young student actor who died on her Majesty's service, who penned the common gossip embarrassing Shakespeare and others, including himself, for falling for the dark, chaste beauty behind the bar? I believe he is a worthy potential candidate, though I will try not to drive myself to despair thinking on it! If Shakespeare did love the fair youth Willobie, he would have been greatly saddened by his death at only twenty followed by the loss of his 11-year-old son five years later. No wonder his sonnets are often preoccupied with death and quests for immortality, be it by passing on one's beauty via offspring or living forever within the sweet witty lines of poetry.

Sonnet 81

Or I shall live your epitaph to make,
Or you survive when I in earth am rotten,
From hence your memory death cannot take,
Although in me each part will be forgotten.
Your name from hence immortal life shall have,
Though I, once gone, to all the world must die:
The earth can yield me but a common grave,
When you entombed in men's eyes shall lie.
Your monument shall be my gentle verse,
Which eyes not yet created shall o'er-read;
And tongues to be your being shall rehearse,
When all the breathers of this world are dead;
You still shall live, such virtue hath my pen,
Where breath most breathes, even in the mouths of men.

24. The King's Arms Or Not The King's Arms

The King's Arms on Oxford's beautiful Broad Street is one of the city's oldest pubs, and is usually packed with students and an ever-increasing number of tourists. There is a local saying that no other pub in England has a higher IQ per square foot than the K.A., though I must point out, this is not always the case at last orders. The popular public house is owned by its neighbour, Wadham College, an establishment with strong ties to King James, who played a small role in the college foundation at the instigation of its co-founder Dorothy Wadham. The pub is thus named after King James and was founded four years after his accession.

There are tales of visiting players having acted in what was the pub's courtyard. Travelling acting troupes generally performed in village halls, pub courtyards and occasionally barns.

Taverns could be rowdy places and were kept outside of the old city walls, away from the University members who lived within the old city walls. There is a legend that the first ever performance of *Hamlet* outside of London, was performed at the King's Arms by the King's men when they toured the university cities of Oxford and Cambridge in 1603. The tour of the university cities is mentioned in the preface of the flimsy piratical quarto addition of *Hamlet*, printed in 1603. I do not doubt that plays were performed at the Kings Arms, all manner of entertainments had commonly disgraced its courtyard including the highly popular and lucrative pastime of Bear baiting, an activity which was strangely allowed to continue in London during the plague epidemics that closed down the theatres. Bare knuckle boxing and cudgel fighting were also popular violent attractions, though at least they didn't involve the abuse of animals. The one vexing problem I have with the legend of this *Hamlet* performance, is that the King's Arms didn't exist until four years after the alleged visit; it opened for trade on September 18th, 1607. A more likely candidate to have hosted this famous courtyard performance would have been the King's head (now called the Crown) which existed a few minutes' walk from the Broad on Cornmarket Street, directly opposite the Crown Inn which Davenant kept and Shakespeare frequented. It too had a reputation for hosting plays and housing players, it also existed within the correct time frame. With both taverns so similarly named it's easy to see how the legend shifted location over time.

However, I endeavoured to discover what existed on the site of the King's Arms pub and if there would have been a building suitable for the showing of plays. I learned from a local fountain of knowledge, Mr John Whitehead, that The King's Arms was built on the site of an old Augustine Friary. To garner a sense of the friary, I decided to take a walk around what is believed to be the perimeter of the old religious house, based on research imparted to me by John Whitehead. The spacious friary would have taken in The King's Arms and its neighbour, Wadham College, it would have also covered the college behind, Harris Manchester, and stretched as far as Rhodes House on Parks Road, around seven acres of land in total. Extensive lawns with picturesque orchards and fruit trees would have existed near Rhodes House. A stroll through Harris Manchester leads to an elegant, clock tower, which has a door dating back to the 15th century, a relic from the friary now embedded within the modern college grounds.[136]

In the late 1530s all friaries, monasteries and nunneries were ransacked and wiped out by Henry VIII's dissolution of the monasteries, led by Thomas Cromwell.

The Austin friary, however, was not in a position to provide rich pickings for the crown; the friars were living in abject poverty, housed in a ruinous building. When a Doctor John London was commissioned to visit the friaries on behalf of Cromwell, their poverty moved him to remark that 'if they do not forsake their houses, their houses will forsake them'. I discovered that the land taken from the Austins changed hands several times before being sold to the city in 1589 by a William Frere who had inherited the site from his parents. It would have been quite unusual during this period for the town to purchase Oxford land as opposed to the university. All I managed to deduce from old records, my walk around the colleges, and a study of the famed Ralph Agas map printed in 1588 (though surveyed a decade earlier) was that only tenements had existed prior to the King's Arms, hardly an ideal location for one to watch a play. However, Dave Richardson, leading light of the Campaign for Real Ale and author of Oxford pubs[137], directed me to search for a framed history of the King's arms, hanging on a wall near the pub's back bar. Having frequented the King's on many occasions I must have walked past the notice of the pub's history hundreds of times, though I must admit, seldom completely sober. It transpires that prior to the King's Arms, an inn called The Lion existed on the very same site, which would certainly appear to be the ideal venue to showcase a play in 17th century Oxford, and I believe that *Hamlet* in 1603 would have been performed at The Lion, giving credence to the King's Arms legend that *Hamlet's* debut performance outside of the capital, took place on the site of the current tavern. Though under an earlier name.

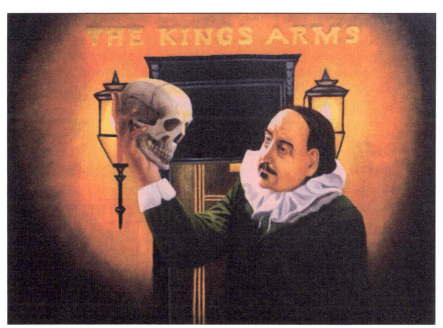

Momento Mori, Hamlet at the Kings arms by Barbara Gorayska

25. Hamlet Must Not Offend Oxford

There are two intriguingly odd name changes in the piratical 1603 quarto edition of *Hamlet*. The self-important know it all, Polonius is changed to Corambis whereas his servant Reynoldo becomes Montano. The Scholar G.R. Hibbard has deduced that the 1603 Quarto edition was probably based on a touring script taken around the Oxbridge cities, with the names changed so not to offend Oxford University which had produced two important scholars with similar sounding names to Polonius and Reynaldo. Polonius sounds incredibly similar to the name of the university's founder Robert Polenius and Reynaldo the servant, too close to the name of the Puritan John Rainolds.[138]

John Rainolds was an important figure at the university at this time and definitely not a man to upset during the players' tour of Oxford. He studied at both Merton and Corpus Christie in his youth and at 54 years of age had been both Dean of Lincoln and Corpus Christie. in 1603 he was about to initiate the creation of the King James authorised version of the Bible. He was Oxford's most prominent Puritan, with a distaste for plays, specifically plays involving what Puritans regarded as the crass act of cross dressing. The boorish puritans also viewed acting as a form of lying, therefore a sin. John Rainolds himself had played the female role of Hippolyta at Oxford for Queen Elizabeth's 1566 visit. It seems time must have hardened his views on the theatre.[139]

Shakespeare knew only too well the perils of upsetting high profile puritans, having already been forced to switch Sir John Oldcastle to Falstaff after Puritan howls of protest. Fortunately for Oxford's visiting players during this period the university chancellor, Thomas Sackville, was 2nd cousin to the Queen. Sackville was a man with a Catholic upbringing and an anti-Puritan outlook, who had also dabbled in poetry and playwriting himself in the 1560s. Nevertheless, it appears the actors played it safe by altering the names for the Oxford performance. This was probably a wise move given that John Rainolds and his Puritan comrades spent the next Christmas at Hampton Court Palace with the monarch, as did the King's men.

Shakespeare's troupe had been promoted to Grooms of the Chamber; they were summoned to Hampton Court as part of the King's entourage.[140] The Puritans were there to discover the true faith of the newly crowned King, who appeased the Puritans on his own terms, with the publication of the King James Bible.

26. A Mouse Trap At Christchurch

Shakespeare's two poems, *The Rape of Lucrece* and *Venus and Adonis* made very popular saucy reading material for the Oxbridge students and certainly helped his career as a playwright, such was the success of Lucrece that it was reprinted nine times throughout his lifetime.

The tale of the student Hamlet, fretting over which move to make next to expose his father's killer was certainly one of the most popular plays amongst the students, with its rollercoaster ride of murders, ghosts and ingenious subplots.

The origins of *Hamlet* date back to early 12th century Icelandic folk tales.

Amleth, a Scandinavian version of the tale was written by Saxo Grammaticus in his *Gesta Danorum* (History of the Danes), a series of sixteen books on the rise and fall of Danish rulers.

Like Hamlet, Amleth feigns madness before taking revenge on his Uncle Fengi, his father's killer. [141]

Shakespeare achieved great success with *Hamlet* around 1601, some four centuries after the Icelandic folk tales were written. There was, however, another play called *Ur Hamlet* doing the rounds of the London theatres in 1589, well over a decade before Shakespeare's *Hamlet*. Unfortunately, there are no surviving copies of *Ur Hamlet*, but a reference to this earlier play displays one clear similarity.

In Wits Miserie and the worlds madness {1596} the religious physician and writer Thomas Lodge compiled a list of 'The Devils Incarnate of this Age', one such Devil he calls Hate-Vertue, it's in the following description of this demon that Lodge references a ghost he saw on stage.

"And though this fiend be begotten of his father's own blood, yet is he different from his nature, & were he not sure the jealousy could not make him a cuckold, he had long since published him for a bastard: you shall know him by this, he is a foul lubber, his tongue tipped with lying, his heart stéeld against charity, he walks for the most part in black under colour of gravity, & looks as pale as the Visard {mask} of the ghost which cried so miserably at the Theatre like an oyster wife, Hamlet, revenge![142]

I believe that an extravagant banquet which took place in Christ Church college June 13th, 1583, was attended by a playwright who not only wrote the 1589 version of *Ur Hamlet* but may well have found inspiration from the actual banquet for a scene similar to the mousetrap sequence.

It is impossible to gauge if Shakespeare was inspired to write the mousetrap scene based on a similar scene in *Ur Hamlet* as there are no surviving copies. There are, however, some surprising similarities between the events of the Christ Church dinner and the famous 'play within a play' scene by which Hamlet witnesses the guilt of his father's killer.

In 1583, The Polish nobleman Albert Laski and revered warlord, made a royal visit to England. A strong broad mountain of a man with a long flowing silver beard, adorned in royal purple velvet robes, Laski certainly must have made an impression on those he encountered. During Laski's visit, Queen Elizabeth was not entirely sure if he was still in favour with the rest of the Polish royal family, he had after all previously attempted to take the crown of Poland by force. Nevertheless, a diplomatic decision was made and the Queen instructed her occasional favourite, Robert Dudley, to organise a series of entertainments to honour the visiting dignitary.

Robert Dudley, The Earl of Leicester was a very powerful right hand man to the Queen, ostensibly the king of middle England. He was instructed to provide the royal barge for a procession along the Thames and then to organize four days of entertainments at the lavish hall of Christ Church college.

Christ Church was a fitting place to hold a royal banquet, a college steeped in Royal history, founded in 1555 as Cardinal College by Wolsey until he fell from King Henry VIIIs favour, it was then briefly renamed King's College before being given its current name.

Robert Dudley, at the time Oxford University chancellor, created the Oxford University Press which he utilized to print anti-Catholic propaganda. Dudley required highly skilled practitioners from the world of theatre to organise the plays to entertain the revellers. He contacted two of his favourite poets of propaganda, William Gager and

George Peele. The playwright George Peele had graduated from Christ Church with an MA in 1579 and was recalled to his old college to direct two plays patched together by his great friend William Gager.

William Gager, in his position as semi-official poet laureate of Christ Church, would often be called upon to knock out a poem or direct a play to commemorate an event such as the death of a noble or, in this case, a regal visit. Familiar with the works of Homer, Virgil and Ovid, there was always a fantastical tale on hand for Gager to call upon at short notice – twenty-six days notice to be precise, for Laski's visit. Gager prepared two plays in great haste for the festivities. He must have been concerned that the plays came across as somewhat rushed; he wrote an epilogue to apologise as much. The two plays chosen were *Rivales* (partially translated from latin by Peele) and a fantasy, *Dido*-translated from Virgil's *Aeneid*

Finding willing Oxford student actors would not have been a problem. The students were on track to become either courtly pen-pushers, priests or lawyers. Acting, or any exercise which required the skills of public oration, were pivotal to their educational progress towards such careers. Peele went all out to impress, devising unique special effects such as sweetmeats falling from the skies.

On June 10th the four day Royal revelry began. Many of England's celebrated poets, scholars, courtiers and wits of the time would have attended the Christ Church entertainments and, as was the case with the celebrated Ben Jonson Masques during the Stuarts' reign, there was diplomatic pressure for these events to impress foreign dignitaries. Nineteen-year-old Shakespeare almost certainly would not have been in attendance.

Laski must have been in his element. Not only was he guest of honour at a Royal banquet in Oxford, he had also met his hero two days earlier, the world famous Alchemist and Royal spiritual advisor John Dee, a mysterious wizard like figure often cited as Shakespeare's model for Prospero.

After two days of partying and fireworks, Albert Laski and his entourage were entertained by the plays on June 13th.

I propose that the ill-fated playwright Thomas Kyd witnessed the plays at the Christ Church banquet and proceeded to write or complete writing *Ur Hamlet*, including a scene inspired by the banquet, which in turn became the basis for the mousetrap plot. It is not improbable Kyd was invited to this grand event by Peele, they clearly knew each other, both London-based playwrights and members of the close-knit and mysterious School of Night.[143]

The School of Night consisted of wits, inventors and explorers who would meet at Sir Walter Raleigh's London residence to discuss worldly matters. Besides Kyd and Peele, the infamous society also included the crypto-Catholic Arts patron Lord Fernando Strange and the enigmatic wizard-like John Dee. [144]

Incidentally, Peele and Kyd have of late, from recent linguistic studies, been linked as probable Shakespeare collaborators; Peele with *Titus Andronicus* and Kyd having been assisted by Shakespeare with his bloody epic, *The Spanish Tragedy*. They were also both co-writers for the Queen's men. The parallels between the onstage melodrama, the audience and the mousetrap scene are fascinating

Enter Robert Dudley as Claudius, watching an ancient story unfold in an exquisite hall, *Dido, Queen of Carthage*, a play which involves the Queen's brother, Pygmallion, secretly murdering his brother-in-law, Dido's husband, for wealth and power. It ends tragically with the suicide of the widowed Queen after her heart is broken by a young gallant, Aeneas. Dido does return in later stories, as a ghost.

Two days before the Oxford trip, Dudley's enemy, the influential Earl of Sussex, died. On his death bed he warned 'beware the gypsy he is too hard for you all'. Dudley was suspected of poisoning Sussex. This suspicious death would have been a common whisper in the close-knit world of court intrigue and likely fresh gossip at the Christ Church banquet. Dudley was already regarded as a ruthless master courtier and was suspected of murdering his own wife, Amy Robsart in 1560 in order to pursue his desire to marry Queen Elizabeth. Poor Amy had apparently fallen a mere five steps to her death on St Michaelmas day, 8th September and suspicion fell upon Dudley when he forced the clergy of the Oxford University church, St Mary's, to bury his wife immediately, without a funeral! Shakespeare's Hamlet speaks the following from an old play which he utilizes to catch out his father's brother as murderer. "One speech in it I chiefly loved: Twas Aeneas tale to Dido and thereabout of it, especially where he speaks of Priam's slaughter. If it live in your memory, begin at this line, Let me see, let me see—

> *The rugged Pyrrhus, like the Hyrcanian beast*
> *It is not so. It begins with Pyrrhus*
> *The rugged Pyrrhus, he whose sable arms,*
> *Black as his purpose, did the night resemble*
> *When he lay couchèd in the ominous horse,*
> *Hath now this dread and black complexion smeared*
> *With heraldry more dismal. Head to foot*
> *Now is he total gules, horridly tricked*
> *With blood of fathers, mothers, daughters, sons*
> *{Hamlet, Act II, Scene II}*

The speech that Hamlet 'chiefly loved' regarding Priam's murder by Pyrrhus as revenge for the death of his father, sets the tone of an old play with subject matters that would make Hamlet's uncle uncomfortable. These themes of murder for personal advancement within the play Dido, may also have made Robert Dudley (Claudius) feel more than a little uncomfortable, especially with rumours circulating over Sussex's death bed accusations.

In attendance at Christ Church was also the Privy Counsellor, the spy master Burghley (Polonius) and of course there was a visiting noble who had seen the battlefield a few times, Albert Laski (Horatio).[145] To quote *Hamlet* 'it was a play not performed often, not for the masses, twas caviar for the General', perhaps General Laski. [146]

When Thomas Lodge referenced the wailing ghost screaming revenge, he didn't mention the identity of the playwright, but many scholars believe that when Thomas Nashe wrote a preface to Robert Greene's *Menaphon* (1589) he not only criticized his contemporaries' writing styles but subtly uncovered Thomas Kyd as the playwright of *Ur Hamlet*. Nashe wrote {Slightly modernised}

> *It is a common practise now a dayes amongst a sort of shifting*
> *companions, that run through every Art and thrive by none,*

*to leave the trade of Noverint, whereto they were borne, and
busy themselves with the endeavours of Art that could scarcely
Latinize their neck verse if they should have need; yet English
Seneca read by Candle-light yields many good sentences,
as Blood is a begger, and so forth; and if you intreate him
faire in a frosty morning, he will afford you whole Hamlets, I
should say handfuls of Tragical speeches. But O griefe! Tempus
edam rerum, what's that will last always? The Sea exhaled
by droppes will in continuance be dry, and Seneca, let blood
line by line and page by page, at length must needes die to our
Stage; which makes his famished followers to imitate the Kid
in Aesop, who, enamoured with the Foxes newfangles, forsook
all hopes of life to leap into a new occupation; and these
men, renouncing all possibilities of credite or estimation, to
intermeddle with Italian Translations: Wherein how poorely
they have plodded, (as those that are neither provincial men,
nor are able to distinguish of Articles,) let all indifferent
Gentlemen that have travelled in that tongue discerned by
their two-pennie Pamphlets.* [147]

In this acerbic paragraph, Thomas Nashe apparently references the play when he remarks that a competitor, one of 'the shifting companions' 'will afoord you whole Hamlets, I should say handfuls of Tragicall speeches'. Many believe that Nashe's puns were aimed at Thomas Kyd, assigning Kyd as the author of *Ur Hamlet*. In agreement with this theory, Sir Sidney Lee remarked that 'when Nash proceeds to point out that Seneca's famished followers imitate 'the Kydde in Aesop' he is apparently punning on the dramatist's name'.[148]

Suppose the angry satirical comments Nashe made were directed at Thomas Kyd, making him the Author of *Ur Hamlet*, the play with the screaming ghost wailing revenge. Assuming Kyd's Hamlet feigns madness as did the Nordic inspiration, Amleth (A Nordic name for insane) then we have a trail of events leading to that great patcher of old plays, Shakespeare and his reworked *Hamlet*.

We will never know for sure if the author of *Ur Hamlet* or *Hamlet* attended the Christ Church banquet in 1583. There are certainly a remarkable number of coincidences to suggest the banquet did partially influence the mousetrap scene in *Hamlet*, but what happened to the guests?

Robert Dudley would never achieve his dream of marrying the Virgin Queen and leaves a legacy steeped in murder and foul play, just like Claudius. Hamlet's home was full of spies, similar to the Privy Council of Queen Elizabeth's. Robert Dudley always signed his letters to Queen Elizabeth with two zeros at the end of his signature to symbolize two watching eyes. John Dee also signed his letters to the Queen adding two zeros followed by the mystical number seven, which incidentally inspired Bond author Ian Fleming to give his international spy the agent number 007.

What happened to the Polish warrior Albert Laski? He was foretold of achieving great wealth by his spiritual hero John Dee but would ironically end his days back in Poland broke, pay-rolling the companionship of John Dee and his shadowy assistant Kelly. [149]

As for Poor Thomas Kyd, he suffered a fate which would have struck terror into the hearts of his peers.

In 1593 'Divers lewd and mutinous libels' had been posted up all over London. On 11 May the Privy Council ordered the arrest of those suspected of such activities. Kyd was one of the unfortunates to be arrested, probably after an informer's tip off. The lodgings he once shared with the tearaway playwright Christopher Marlowe were searched and though mutinous libels were not found, atheist literature was discovered, including writings claiming Jesus Christ was a homosexual. After being subjected to brutal torture on the rack, Kyd broke down and told the Privy Council that his former roommate Marlowe was the producer of the controversial papers. Not long after being summoned by the Privy Council and whilst awaiting their decision, Marlowe was fatally stabbed in the eye by known government agents during a fight at an inn, though this was likely to have been an assassination covered up as a bar room brawl. Kyd was never the same after his horrendous ordeal on the rack. He died a broken man a year after his torture, aged only 35,[150] a stark warning of the perils of being a playwright in Elizabethan times, when the streets of London were riddled with spymasters and informers. Just like Hamlet's castle.

27. Oriel

Behind The gigantic splendour of Christ Church and opposite Corpus Christie lies Oriel college, a pretty establishment with foundations dating back to 1324.

Oriel college could be considered, for many reasons, as the bad boy of Oxford colleges, a college happy to go against the grain of public opinion.

One controversial example of their diffident outlook is when the 2015–2016 'Rhodes must fall' campaign gathered mass momentum with the Oxford university student union, the union's deafening demands to have the statue of colonial iconoclast, Cecil Rhodes removed, fell onto deaf ears as Oriel, in typically grim defiance, simply wouldn't listen.

There is, however, an earlier incident in the resume of Oriel's bad boy achievements, one that would offend the sensibilities of any librarian.

After the heroic success of the Oxford men to save the Bodleian first folio in the early 20th century, it is disheartening to learn that Oriel actually sold their own first folio as recently as 2003. This affair was brought to my attention by a previous college member, my source however wishes to remain anonymous.

This Oxford tragedy apparently began as the result of some botched cleaning of an old Oriel hall in which dirt that had kept the building together was removed, resulting in the hall's state of disrepair. Short on funds, a decision was reached by the bursar and the governing body to discreetly sell their prized first folio, a near perfect copy, still with its original bindings. The book was given to the college in 1786 by a former undergraduate Lord Leigh. Leigh was a prolific donator of money and books to his former college, a generous man who suffered periods of severe mental illness, sectioned on numerous occasions. Word of this sale spread to the college's alumni over a sad weekend in March via a Telegraph newspaper cutting pinned up on the common room notice board, much to the dismay of the college members. 'College sells first folio of the Bard to pay bills' read the headline. The article stated that the antiquarian book keeper, Sir John Paul Getty, was delighted to have bought the book for £3.5 million, a deal concluded in New York. Though Getty had near intact second, third and fourth folios, the first edition had so far escaped him. The secrecy of this sell off, according to my source, brought with it an ill feeling within the common room.

It is alleged that Oriel staff were initially informed that the copy auctioned off was not the Lord Leigh version. However, this was found to be false, as Leigh's markings were plain to see, which intensified feelings of mistrust regarding the handling of the college's affairs. The reaction from one old boy was to retract capital he had planned to leave to the college in his will. 'Building repairs and text books' was the reason given for the controversial sell off. According to my mole, the college invested money from the sale into a 'rundown business park in Cheltenham' to bring in revenue. Perhaps the acts of generosity displayed by the troubled Lord Leigh may have been literally moments of madness, perhaps the same could be said of Oriel's decision to let the first folio go. A week later, another newspaper cutting was pinned onto the common room notice board which read 'John Paul Getty saves book for the nation'.

Though the book was valued in New York and the deal concluded there, it was brought back to England and now resides in John Paul Getty's Oxfordshire manor house, not a million miles from Oriel, though that may be scant consolation to the college members. Unfortunately, Sir John Paul Getty didn't have much of an opportunity to enjoy his greatest purchase as he died just six weeks later.

28. The Merry Wives Of. . . Abingdon?

In the preface of Nicholas Rowe's biography[151] of Shakespeare, he stated that Queen Elizabeth 'was so well pleased with that admiral character of Falstaff in the two parts of Henry the fourth that she commanded him to continue in it for one more play, and to show him in love'. Rowe may well have picked this tale up from the playwright John Dennis[152]. In Dennis's 1702 adaptation of the *Merry Wives of Windsor*, *The Comical Gallant*, he wrote in the introduction that The Merry Wives 'pleased one of the greatest queens that ever was in the world… This comedy was written at her command, and by her direction, and she was so eager to see it acted that she commanded it to be finished in fourteen days.'[153] It is quite an unusual story that the Queen would command Shakespeare to write a story featuring Sir John Falstaff in love, so unusual that it is probably more likely an event to have happened than to been made up. If the Queen was a great fan of Falstaff (and who can blame her) then it would probably have come as a great relief given the complaints from court over Falstaff's modelling on the Puritan Sir John Oldcastle.

Was fourteen days enough time for even Shakespeare to write such a comedy? Speculation over the centuries alludes to Shakespeare that great patcher-upper of old plays, to have garnered inspiration from Oxford playwright, Henry Porter's *The Two Angry women of Abingdon*.[154]

Abingdon, a small market town, just over 5 miles south of Oxford, with a population of around 30,000, has the distinction of being the oldest recorded settlement in England. A quaint place by day, it has a reputation of being quite rowdy at night. It is clear that Henry Porter knew Abingdon and the Oxford area rather well, knowing that the Carfax area in Oxford housed the city church of St Martin's where many nobles would have wed. The London Theatre manager and impresario Philip Henslowe lists Porter as not only a gentleman but also a poor scholar, so it is assumed with little conviction that he was an Oxford scholar though there are no college records to back this up. He may well have been an Oxford-born man, especially given his perceived knowledge of Abingdon. Henslowe also records many payments in 1598 for the play and its costumes, though the play can be dated to pre-1590 as there are references to some of the leading characters in a 1589 pamphlet entitled *Plaine Percevall*.

The madcap play centres around two women who dislike each other, jealous Mistress Barnes who mistakenly believes Mistress Goursey to be having an affair with her husband. The two husbands, in an attempt to force their bickering wives to be civil, try to arrange a marriage between their respective offspring, Mall Barnes and Frank Goursey, which inevitably and eventually leads to all types of chaos with the many quarrelling parties chasing each other blindly through the woods during a pitch black night.

Entered into this fray are many eccentric characters such as Barnes' servant Nicholas who answers only in proverbs, much to the mockery of his neighbours. There is a hard drinking comical figure, a servant to the Gourseys, who claims to have travelled the world, Dick Coombes, a man who boasts in a rather Sir John Falstaff manner, 'Tis no consequent to me: you know I have drunk all the alehouses in Abington dry', which brought to my mind a few Abingdon folk I know. Interestingly, Sir John is randomly mentioned in a speech from Dick Coombes when he compares gold to women, having been offered money by Mistress Goursey to fight Mistress Barnes' servants:

> But this is a miracle to me, that gold that is heavy hath
> the upper, and a woman that is light doth soonest fall,
> considering that light things aspire, and heavy things soonest
> go down: but leave these considerations to Sir John; they
> become a black-coat better than a blue. Well, mistress, I had
> no mind to-day to quarrel;
> but a woman is made to be a man's seducer; you say, quarrel?

Shakespeare may have even found inspiration for the title of one of his plays from the following speech when Master Goursey expresses his anger at having to near beg his wife to not read one of his private letters.

> I did not think, good faith, I could have set
> So sour a face upon it, and to her,
> My bed-embracer, my right bosom friend.
> I would not that she should have seen the letter—
> As poor a man as I am—by my troth,
> For twenty pound: well, I am glad I have it. [Aside.]
> Ha, here's ado about a thing of nothing!

The *Merry Wives of Windsor* and *The Two Angry Women of Abingdon* have many similarities: jealous partners, Master Ford in Windsor and Mistress Barnes in Abingdon; an arranged marriage which many fall out over violently, centred around a 17 year old maiden, Anne Page in Windsor, Mall Barnes in Abingdon; Abingdon has Dick Coombes, a man with a Falstaffian appetite for boozing who is proud in demeanour but often ends up the butt of jokes. Coombes falls into a pond, Falstaff's thrown into the Thames. Both plays are set in the countryside, incredibly funny, full of sharp wit and both climax with chaotic scenes at night time in the woods.

It is conceivable that Shakespeare may have been inspired by *The Two Angry Women*, an ideal play to garner material, especially if the legend is true regarding the Queen's short notice command for Shakespeare to produce *Merry Wives*. Another play Porter wrote that must have inspired Shakespeare's title was the *Four Merry Women of Abingdon*, a play which unfortunately has disappeared along with all of Porter's solo efforts bar *The Two Angry Women*. It is a great shame that Porter's other plays are no longer extant as *The Two Angry Women* is an exceptionally funny play and I would suggest well worth reprising for the stage. His comedic talents were recognised in the Francis Meres manuscript *Paladis Tamia*, the same book that mentioned honey tounged Shakespeare. Francis Meres described Porter as 'the best for Comedy amongst us'. Porter was ranked highly enough by his peers to have collaborated with the cream of London based talent, Ben Jonson, Henry Chettle and, if we are to believe modern linguistic technology, Christopher Marlowe on some of the Doctor Faust comedic scenes.[155]

Unfortunately, as was often the case for many a 16th century playwright, Porter's last years were spent in debt and the last financial record regarding him is in Henslowe's Diary, 26th May 1599 – sadly not a payment to the playwright but an IOU to the theatre manager.[156] There is a passage, spoken by the servant Dick Coombe, that seems rather poignant.

> *I see by this dearth of good swords, that dearth of sword-and-*
> *buckler fight begins to grow out: I am sorry for it; I shall*
> *never see good manhood again, if it be once gone; this poking*
> *fight of rapier and dagger will come up then; then a man, a*
> *tall man, and a good sword-and-buckler man, will be spitted*
> *like a cat or a coney; then a boy will be as good as a man,*
> *unless the Lord show mercy unto us*

Mercy must have been an alien concept during the last fortnight of poor Henry Porter's life as ten days after the IOU had been written, he was stabbed to death in Southwark by another Playwright, John Day. Porter was recorded as having been struck a mortal wound on the left breast with a rapier, ironically the fashionable and dangerous weapon Dick Coombes complained about. The murderer John Day was arrested but given a Royal pardon, having been charged with murder, he admitted manslaughter on grounds of self-defence. 'A rogue and a base fellow' was how Jonson described him. Day had a murky past, having been expelled from Cambridge in 1593 for book theft. He ended his days sleeping rough at Beggar's Bush [157] Then again, he also worked for Henslowe, an unscrupulous business man, not famed for generous wage packets. No wonder Shakespeare and friends became their own theatre managers.

29. Tears In The Town Hall

On the anniversary of Shakespeare's birthday, a lovely tradition has been started over the last few years by the Oxford Preservation Trust. Children from various schools partake in performing excerpts from *Othello* in the Oxford Town hall. The Town hall is built on the site of the Guildhall which hosted the King's Men's performance of *Othello*, sometime in September 1610. Thomas Harris, the Lord Mayor was in charge of organizing payment as the play was paid for by the local authorities, not the University. At this time, University members were banned from attending plays by professional playing companies. Oxford students were occasionally banned from playing football in the middle ages, but it would be naive to believe a football wasn't booted during the ban and thus it's safe to say some University students did attend this performance of *Othello*, an unusual Oxford audience consisting of a unique blend of locals and students; two factions that seldom saw eye to eye.

A King's men production of Ben Jonson's brutally satirical, anti-Puritan masterpiece, *The Alchemist*, upset some of the scholars. Their version of *Othello*, however, went down a storm; the tragic murder of Desdemona drawing tears from the eyes of those in attendance.[158]

Perhaps Oxford audiences were a sensitive lot, forty years after *Othello* had moved the Oxford men to sob, audience members in the big bad City of London were privy to a production wherein some of the crowd were not quite so sensitive, as Samuel Pepys testified in his diary, in which he recalled 'a very pretty lady sat by me and called out to see Desdemona smothered'.

30. Master William Peter - Oblivion In The Darkest Day To Come

It's only been widely accepted within the last two decades that Shakespeare collaborated often with other playwrights, especially near the end of his career. Various linguistic forensic scientific methods have been applied using sophisticated computer technology to trace patterns in the writing styles of playwrights. The fascinating results from these methods have dramatically altered the way we look at Shakespeare's works and his standing as a lone genius. These results suggest that George Wilkins wrote much of *Titus Andronicus* and that Shakespeare may have actually written segments of the hugely successful revenge drama, *The Spanish Tragedy*, a play for centuries attributed solely to Thomas Kyd. Another play actually re-attributed to Shakespeare in recent years is the brutal Yorkshire Tragedy, believed to be a collaboration between Shakespeare and Thomas Middleton.[159]

The Shakespeare apocrypha contains many plays and sonnets that at have some stage been attributed to Shakespeare, often without universal acceptance and in some cases with deliberately false attribution employed by publishers eager to cash in on Shakespeare's success. For example, the 16th century pirate of publishing, William Jaggard, in 1599, printed a collection of twenty poems entitled *The Passionate Pilgrim* by W.S. Shakespeare, of which we know only five of these poems are authentically Shakespearean.

Though the Jaggard example is from Shakespeare's lifetime, modern linguistic forensics have recently brought to light some fascinating additions to the murky world of the Shakespeare apocrypha, one of these additions involves a tribute to an Oxford student.

On the 13th of February 1612, Thomas Thorpe – the man who published Shakespeare's sonnets –registered with the stationer's guild, *A funeral elegy in memory of the late virtuous Master William Peter by W.S.* dedicated to his older brother and Oxford University dropout John Peter.[160] The poem is rather long at 4,600 words and relentless in its high appraisal of the late William Peter, it is peppered with over the top praises such as 'a life free from such stains as follies are' and 'as that his virtue was his best attire.' The overly-long poem, reminds me somewhat of attending a church service as a child, listening impatiently to a sermon that makes you wish you had painted eyes on your lids to appear awake. There is, however, a purpose behind the incessant nature of the complimentary tributes, and that was to paint a sheen over the rather inglorious end to the former Oxford student.

The Funeral Elegy was brought to the attention of the public by Don Foster, a professor of English literature at Vassar College in the United States. Foster is one of the world's leading experts in the field of literary forensics, divulging that "no two people use language in precisely the same way, our identities are encoded in our own language, in a kind of literary DNA." Foster's unique skills have enabled him to unmask anonymous authors. The press have described him as "a literary sleuth",[161] the FBI and the police have hired Foster to unmask the identities of blackmailers and terrorists.[162] During the winter of 1984, Foster was studying a microfilm collection of early English books from 1475 to 1640 in order to learn something of the literature of the time prior to writing a dissertation on the sonnets. During his studies he came across the aforementioned Funeral Elegy signed by W.S. The professor was startled by the poet's dedicatory epistle and its similarity to Shakespeare's dedication in *The Rape of Lucrece*.[163]

The intrigue grew in momentum when Foster noticed what he felt to be Shakespearian echoes throughout the elegy.

One example that Foster gives is the similarity between Richard II's last speech to his wife and the prediction W.S. makes that Peter's death will cause much sorrow.[164]

> *Let them tell thee tales*
> *Of woeful ages long ago betid*
> *And ere thou bid good night, to quit their griefs*
> *Tell thou the lamentable tale of me*
> *And send the hearers weeping to their beds*
> ***[Richard II 5.1.41-45]***

> *Such as do recount that tale of woe*
> *Told by remembrance of the wisest heads*
> *Will in the end conclude the matter so,*
> *As they will all go weeping to their beds*
> ***[Elegy, lines 167-70]***

Convinced he had discovered a lost work of Shakespeare, the intrepid professor travelled across the pond to visit both Exeter and Oxford to learn more about the tragic man eulogised in the poem.

We know from Foster's in depth investigations that William Peter was born in 1582 in Devon to Devonshire gentry. He became an Oxford scholar, matriculating at the college which favoured West Country scholars, Exeter College, Lincoln College being the hub for students from Lincolnshire etc. He studied at Oxford for nine years. After leaving Oxford, twenty-six-year-old Peter married seventeen-year-old Margaret

Bruton (alias Breton) in Shillingford St. George on January 9th, 1608/9. Margaret grew up in the shadow of Penslow Priory near land which the Peters had owned for decades. The year before the marriage saw the death of both Will and Margaret's parents, which implies they were both financially secure and not marrying to gain social advantage.

The most information we have regarding the personality traits of William Peter are garnered from an account complied by Exeter's City recorder William Martyn just hours after Peters death, the verdict details the events which resulted in-to quote the author W. S 'Oblivion in the darkest day to come'.

On January 25th, 1612 William Peter of Whipton was the victim of a violent murder. He was only twenty-nine years old, not long married and recently a father.

The wintery day's events which led to Peter's untimely death began at ten in the morning, with two wealthy brothers, John and Edward Drew, riding together from their Killerton estate for a day of tavern hopping throughout Exeter. The first watering hole they reached was called the Oxford Inn. The host of the establishment, Giles Geal, offered to sell Edward 'a fine looking pony'. A horse trading enthusiast, Edward was given permission to take the horse for a ride.

John Drew remained at the tavern upon hearing that his brother was riding to Will Peter's house to 'make a quarrel with him about the buying of a horse'. Edward was unhappy that Will Peter had snitched on him to his mother, informing Lady Drew that her son had borrowed money for a horse from 'old Mr.Halse' without paying the man back. The news of Edwards nefarious activities would have gone down like a lead balloon in the Drew family household, especially as Edward had recently been excommunicated from Oxford University for defrauding an Oxford merchant.

Edward arrived at Will Peter's house with a smile and urged Peter to join him and his brother for a few pots of beer. Over the course of the day the brothers and Will Peter visited six different public houses. Whilst drinking copiously throughout the day, Edwards behaviour became increasingly troublesome. At the second tavern, Will was pestered by Edward to sell him his horse, which he wouldn't. Later, at the Bear Inn, Edward threatened to throw biscuits onto the floor if the hostess dared to place them onto his table. He then proceeded to 'talk very wantonly' with her. Fortunately, Will intervened. Many pots of beer and several bottles of Canary wine later, at the Mermaid tavern, Edward spewed beer onto a house of cards that one of the servants had been building. This led to a temporary shoving match between Will and Edward,

Half an hour later and near seven o clock, all three acquaintances were on horseback in the yard of the Mermaid, drinking more beer in the lamplight when they were joined by another local. Without words being exchanged Will and Edward crossed their horses several times to prevent each other from leaving, Will must have felt uncomfortable as he bolted off only to be chased through the dark streets of Exeter by a manic Edward Drew – brother John's horse simply couldn't keep pace.

When Edward caught up with Will he thrust his sword through the back of his skull with such force that the tip pierced the brain, he left his victim on the ground claiming to his brother that Will must have fallen. Later that night, in the room the brothers shared, Edward told John "I pray God Master Peter be well." The next morning Edward was arrested for the murder of Will Peter.[165]

From this post-mortem, a fascinatingly detailed picture is painted of two contrasting personalities, Will Peter, family man, honest to a fault, constantly intervening when Edward Drew's embarrassing behaviour became threatening, even informing Edward's mother of his duplicitous dealings. Edward on the other hand, a real bad egg, immature and still sharing a room with his brother, ripping off merchants and friends even after his expulsion from Oxford and then ferociously slaughtering Will, a family friend.

Justice was served and twenty men who sat on the coroner's jury returned an indictment of 'wilful murder.' However, the trial was deferred until May, by which time Edward had broken out of jail and fled to Virginia, not only a popular settlement for the pilgrim fathers but a refuge for English criminals on the run.[166]

When Don Foster made his 'discovery' public in 1995 it made the New York times front page – though it didn't impress respected Shakespeare scholars including Stanley Wells (too boring to be Shakespeare) or Katherine Duncan Jones.[167] The Funeral Elegy did, however, make its way into three different editions of Shakespeare's complete works.

Alas in 2002 a group of literary scholars, Professor Brian Vickers, Richard Kennedy and Professor Gilles D. Monsarrat produced enough evidence to claim that the likely writer of the eulogy was Will Peter's fellow Exeter college member and Devonshire neighbour John Ford, famed writer of the popular *Tis pity she's a whore*. Ford's poem *Christ's bloody sweat* had so many similarities to the *Funeral Elegy* that Don Foster and his supporters had to admit defeat, though Foster's recantation was exceptionally gracious when he stated "No one who cannot rejoice in the discovery of his own mistakes deserves to be called a scholar."[168]

Why was the dedication signed by W.S.? perhaps another attempt by an opportunist publisher (Thomas Thorpe) to make some extra income by attaching the initials of the more popular William Shakespeare.

Some observers also thought It rather unlikely that Shakespeare would have been in the right frame of mind to compose the *Funeral Elegy* considering his brother, the unsuccessful actor Edmund Shakespeare had died less than a fortnight earlier.

It is, however, from Foster's incredibly thorough research that we have learned that Edward Drew, William Shakespeare and William Peter shared many friendships. William Peter was related to a Thomas Russell, close friend of Shakespeare and overseer of his will, also related to Henry Willoughby, the Oxford student connected in many ways to Shakespeare. Shakespeare's writing partner Francis Beaumont had grown up with Edward Drew, and the Devonshire friend of Will Peter, former Oxford student and the Funeral Elegy author John Ford also wrote for the King's men theatre company.[169]

In 2002, whilst commenting on Brian Vickers' victorious proposal for John Ford, an interesting connection was made by Don Foster's supporter Professor Richard Abrams[170], of the University of Southern Maine, that Will Peter and his elder brother John both attended Exeter College as did their second cousin, once removed, Sir William Petre II.[171] Sir Petre was a larger than life character who was immortalised in poetry by the talented Edmund Spencer. He was also closely connected to the two likeliest candidates for Shakespeare's patronage, friends with Southampton and related to Pembroke through marriage. It is known that this flamboyant relative of the Peters participated in Royal masques and very much enjoyed the atmosphere of the famous Mermaid Tavern on the Cheapside in London.[172]

If John Ford wrote the Funeral Elegy he probably did so in London. Ford was also a known frequenter of the Mermaid. It is not unlikely given the evidence we now have (thanks to Don Foster's research) based on shared acquaintances, that William

Petre, John Ford and Shakespeare may well have raised a toast to the tragic former Oxonian William Peter, in the legendary Mermaid Tavern, absolutely teeming with the great dramatists and creative wits of the time.

31. Three Scholars And A Mermaid

It could be said that Shakespeare's lack of formal education may have actually given him an advantage. His phraseology was much more naturalistic than his peers,[173] less pompous and without the grandiose lyrical pomp of a Christopher Marlowe. Smug Jonson regarded himself as more witty and cultured than Shakespeare with his 'small Greek and little Latin'[174], but the facts speak for themselves and the fame of Shakespeare's lines tower over his contemporaries. Most people, without the slightest interest in the theatre would be familiar with

> *'O Romeo, Romeo —wherefore art thou Romeo,'*
> **(Romeo & Juliet, Act II, Scene II)**
> *'To be or not to be – that is the question',*
> **(Hamlet Act III, scene I)**
>
> *'A horse, a horse, my kingdom for a horse,'*
> **(Richard III, Act V, Scene IV)**
>
> *'Friends, Romans, countrymen, lend me your ears'*
> **(Julius Caesar, Act III, Scene II)**

The same cannot be said for the speeches of Jonson or Marlowe. Even more interestingly, the plays of Jonson, Beaumont and Fletcher were all the rage for decades after the Bard's death, while Shakespeare became something of a forgotten playwright.

The most studied man in English literature the world over never attended university and though his audacity to invade the market reserved for the Oxbridge Alumni initially prompted bitterness and resentment from the likes of Robert Greene, the praise from students themselves in his own lifetime would have given Shakespeare much cheer. His erotic poems and his play about the troubled Danish student Hamlet made him the students' favourite playwright. Tributes in the first folio to the late poet were all from educated men, including three younger Oxford scholars James Mabbe, Hugh Holland and Leonard Digges,[175] the latter having close family connections with Shakespeare.

Though we cannot be sure for certain if they rendezvoused with their hero in Oxford, we do know that they were partial to a few beers at the bard's London local, the Mermaid Tavern, a most popular drinking hole located east of St Paul's Cathedral and a drunken haven for poets, players and secret Catholics.(Mermaid regular Ben Jonson filled all three of those roles.) The three Oxford scholars' tributes all allude to the creation of the folio as an immortalisation of Shakespeare. James Mabbe was a Magdalen College fellow and a respected poet, renowned for his literary translations from Spanish into English, particularly the works of Cervantes. He wrote, rather morbidly, 'wee wondered Shakespeare - that thou wenst so soon. From the worlds stage - to the graves Tyring room.' Hugh Holland's main claim to fame actually is his tribute to Shakespeare. A Cambridge student who was later associated with Balliol at

Oxford, he was a poet well versed in the classics and an experienced traveller. His loose tongue often landed him in hot water. One such case involved making derogatory comments about the Queen whilst in Rome, only to be sternly reprimanded by the British ambassador as he passed through Constantinople. His tribute included these prophetic lines, 'for though his line of life went soone about, the life yet of his lines shall never out.' University college graduate Leonard Digges was the third Oxford man to become part of this esteemed literary circle. Leonard and his accomplished family were closely acquainted with Shakespeare. Leonard's father of the same name was a famous astronomer with a claim to have invented the first telescope. When his father died, Leonard's mother remarried a Thomas Russell of Alderminster. Leonard's stepfather, Stratford native Russell, must have been close to Shakespeare as he was asked to be one of the overseers of his will, in which he was left £5. In the small world of Jacobean England Thomas Russell's sister-in-law married William Willobie, older brother of Henry, Digges, like Mabbe, was a Hispanist and a 'minor poet'. His tribute included these lines which sum up the legacy of Shakespeare's first published collection of plays. 'This book, when brass and marble fade, shall make thee look fresh to all ages.'

And that is a sentiment we cannot argue with !

Epilogue

It would be ridiculous for Oxford to boast of Shakespeare's links to the City as a main centre piece for tourism and local interest, though just as ridiculous is that Shakespeare's Oxford links have been so incredibly overlooked, Oxford goes through ebbs and flows of celebrating the National poets connections to Oxford, which as Dr Emma Smith correctly points out were more town than gown.[176]

It is a great shame, however, that the painted room is not open to the public on a regular basis, it is perhaps not the easiest place to attract visitors, an uninviting doorway leads to a series of winding narrow steps which takes one past a noisy bookmakers before reaching the small and fragile room. The beautifully preserved wall paintings were rediscovered behind wooden panels in the early 1900s, and their discovery stirred interest in the Shakespeare and Oxford connections, a copycat of the Stratford tradition of celebrating Shakespeare's official birthday with a procession began in Oxford in 1938, the City and University dignitaries marched from the Town hall to sup Sack in the overcrowded painted room, this tradition which died out in the 1960s has been resurrected since 2013 with the majority of the procession involving school children- and consequently a lot less Sack !![177]

Oxford University will always boast some of the world's leading Shakespearean scholars and the great number of local and visiting theatre companies mean you could watch at least twenty different Shakespeare productions a year without stepping out of Oxford.

I sincerely hope that this project has entertained and enlightened people to what I believe to be an underemphasised area of Shakespearean biography and how the combination of the legends, rumours and events that I have regaled in this book, may have shaped Shakespeare's works and life.

Throughout my studies I was surprised by a grim pattern which emerged; the prolific amount of murders from sharp blades Elizabethan actors, playwrights and gentry succumbed to. In this book alone the body pile up includes William Knell, Henry Porter, Christopher Marlowe and William Peter. Even William Davenant the poet laureate once thrust a rapier into a man who mocked his appearance.

The links that I have found particularly interesting during my research are the many and varied connections between Shakespeare, Henry Willobie, Thomas Russell, Leonard Digges and the murdered Exeter man William Peter. A study into Shakespeare's times certainly reveals a surprisingly small world, buzzing with a cross pollination of artistic and forward thinking creatives, setting the stage for successive generations to tread upon.

Notes

1. Jonathan Bates, *The Genius of Shakespeare*, Picador, London 1998 and 2008,
P.200 A classic example from Bates regarding Shakespeare's remodelling to suit a political agenda is Tory politician Michael Portillo's reading of Ulysses speech {Troilus and Cressida} in defence of established British institutions.

2. Shakespeare, *The Tempest* , Act V, Scene I,
Famous quote from Miranda "O brave new world that has such people in it"

3. Raphael Holinshed, *Holinshed chronicles*, 1577,
Holinshed was one of the main contributors to the historic chronicles of England, Scotland and Ireland, a project initially instigated by printer Reyner Wolfe as an ambitious history of the entire world.

4. Paul Collins, *The book of WILLIAM, How Shakespeare's first folio conquered the world*, New York, USA 2009
P.99 Collins remarks on Samuel Jonson's astute observation

5. Ibid, P100, Collins gives a brilliant account of the great work of Garrick in popularising Shakespeare.

6. Gregory Doran, *Shakespeare's lost play, Finding Cardenio* by Gregory Doran, London, Nick Hern books 2012

7. Bill Bryson *Shakespeare, The World's a stage* Harper Collins 2007
P.27-Bryson's superb book gives one an interesting insight into the diet of the English during Shakespeare's lifetime, including the fact that ale was drank with breakfast

8. Local historians Chris Peters, Dan Glazebrook and John Whitehead were all very helpful regarding the Players Oxford visits

9. Dr Emma Smith, *A treasure lost and regained* , November 11th, 2011, Lecture at the Bodleian library,

10. Jonathan Bate, *The genius of Shakespeare*, London, Picador, 2008 ,
P.352 Greene's warning to his fellow Oxbridge writers

11. Simon Image, An Oxford historian is one who believes Shakespeare may have been too embarrassed at first to reveal himself as a writer.

12. Peter Ackroyd, *Shakespeare the Biography*, London, Random house, {2005}
P.445 Ackroyd details one account of Shakespeare suing a neighbour

13. Ibid p.96 Ackroyd mentions Stratford's visiting player companies

14. Mary Ellen Snodgrass, *World clothing and fashion, An Encyclopedia of history, culture and social influence* Abingdon, Routledge, 2015
P.415 –Tarleton's influence on popular culture.

15. Katherine Duncan Jones, *Shakespeare, An Ungentle life*, London ,A & C Publishers ltd,{2010}
P.34 Praise from Nashe and Heywood for Knells acting skills

16. Jonathan Bate, T*he Genius of Shakespeare* ,
P.134 William Knells death, the oft mentioned notion of Shakespeare taking his place.

17. www.Thametowncouncil.gov.uk 2014 –{author unlisted}
Provides an interesting insight into the local 16th century murder of William Knell

18. Michael Wood, *In Search of Shakespeare Episode 1*, BBC,
The similarity to the Queens men's repertoire and The famous Shakespeare canon is mentioned by Wadham college man Michael Wood in his brilliant documentary series

19. Peter Ackroyd –*Shakespeare the Biography*,
 P.141 The list of the acting companies Shakespeare had joined

20. Extremely informative Stratford upon Avon walking tour guide known as Jan, listed in great detail the goods carriers transported, if in Stratford I highly recommend the tour.

21. GB Historical GIS / University of Portsmouth, History of Grendon Underwood, in Aylesbury Vale and Buckinghamshire | Map and description, *A Vision of Britain through Time*.
URL: http://www.visionofbritain.org.uk/place/1491
Reference to the strange rhyme about the area

22. Abigail Saltmarsh, *New York Times* November 24th 2011-
 Informative travel article on the Elizabethan house, complete with a legend of Shakespeare's ghost

23. Sally Shalam *The Guardian* 22nd November 2008,
 Another informative article regarding Shakespeare's visits to Grendon Underwood

24. John Marston, *Jack drums entertainment,* a play published by Richard Olive 1601

25. Martin Thomas www.Banburymuseum.org

26. Catherine Wolfe-Smith, Local tour guide has been very helpful regarding the history of old wall paintings and the painted room.

27. Mary Edmond, *Rare Sir William Davenant, Poet Laureate-Playwright-Civil war General-Restoration theatre manager-* Manchester, Manchester University Press,1987
P.23 Tattletons tenure and The New College inventory

28. Ibid P.11

29. Ibid, P.12

30. Ibid P.23, Edmond makes interesting connections between the Davenant and Donne families

31. Ibid P.7-9 Connections between Davenant's family and Shakespeare's circle

32. Ibid P.19 Underhill connection

33. Ibid P.21 Underhill connections continued, supposition of advice to Davenant to take on the Crown

34. Ibid P.13 Earliest reference to the Davenants living in Oxford

35. John Aubrey, *Brief Lives*, Hampshire, The Folio society limited,{1979} P.98

36. Mary Edmond, *Rare Sir William*,
P.13 Woods corroboration with Aubrey

37. David Hill Radcliffe, *Spencer and the tradition, English poetry 1579-1840*, www.spensereans.cath.vt.edu

38. William Shakespeare, *As You like it* , Act 2, scene 5,
Jaques "I can *suck melancholy out of a song* as a weasel sucks eggs"

39. Ben Jonson, *Every man and his humour*, 1598

40. Declan McHugh –Jonson's comic putdown was regaled during McHugh's highly recommended Shakespeare in the City walking tour in London, Blackfriars

41. Mary Edmond, Rare Sir William, P.24

42. Ibid, P.23,

43. Ibid, P.24

44. Ibid .P.25, Anonymous poetic tributes to John Davenant

45. Germaine Greer, *Shakespeare's wife*, New York, Harper Collins Publishers 2007,
P.7 One of numerous examples of Shakespeare's wife's reputation sullied in literature, in this occasion by James Joyce.

46. Schoenbaum, *Shakespeare lives* 1970 reprinted by Oxford University press 1993

47. Saul Isler, *Shakespeare is missing*, an Ovid Kent novel, XLIBRIS September 20,2013

48. Mary Edmond, *Rare Sir William*,
P.15 Edmond gives examples of Authors over the centuries romanticising the links between Jennet and William Shakespeare including Arthur H Nethercot's "William Shakespeare" 1938, Sir Walter Scott's "Woodstock" 1826 and Gorge Bernard Shaw's "The dark lady of the sonnets" 1908, I have added a few more writers to the examples Edmond provided.

49. Henry Willobie, Charles Hughes, *Willobie his Avisa with an essay towards its interprtation*, Miami USA, HardPress publishing
P.9-P.11 Publication date, details of Dorrell's "discovery"

50. Ibid P.20 Shakespeare's advice

51. Ibid P.9 Earliest references to Shakespeare

52. Steven Trotter, *The Shakespeare code Willobie his Avisa decoded, an introduction* September 24th 2013, https://theshakespearecode.wordpress.com/2013/09/24/willobie-his-avisa-decoded-part-one/
Information regarding The banning of Willobie his Avisa

53. Ibid P.159 Penelope's complaint

54. Ibid P.23 The war in Hungary

55. Mary Edmond, Rare Sir William, p.31

56. Ibid P.40

57. Ibid P.44-45 William Davenant's misfortune with venereal disease

58. Ibid P.55- 59, Davenant's rise as master of the court masques

59. Ibid P.87- 88 The army plot

60. Ibid P.91 The Puritans destruction of the theatres

61. Ibid P.96 Edmonds gives detailed information on the honours Davenant received

62. Ibid P.103

63. Ibid P.116

64. Ibid, P.112 One of the ever enterprising and crafty innovator's successful schemes to bypass the Puritans strict rules

65. Ibid P.130 Another of Davenant's ground breaking changes to the stage

66. Ibid P.142

67. Ibid. P.148

68. Ibid, P.150 Pepys praise for Betterton whom he named his pet dog after

69. Ibid. P166

70. Ibid, P.159 Davenant's innovative changes to the theatre

71. Ibid P.169

72. Ibid, P.185

73. Ibid P.198

74. Ibid P.199

75. Ibid, P.70 Epitaph for Davenant inspired by Jonsons

76. Peter Ackroyd, *Shakespeare, the Biography*
P.34-35 Excellent account of Shakespeare's Catholic inclined homeland

77. Ibid P.94 *The end of Somerville and family*

78. Ibid P.61 Detailed account of Shakespeare's Catholic teachers

79. Ibid P.67-68 Richard Davies early writings on Shakespeare

80. Ibid, P.68 Woods suppositions that Richard Davies was drunk whilst writing of Shakespeare's misspent youth

81. Joe Egerton, *A Jesuit for today* http://www.thinkingfaith.org/articles/20100414_1.htm 14th April 2010

82. Michael L Carafiello, *Robert Parsons and English Catholicism*, 1994 P.15, Strained relations with Squire and Bagshaw

83. Ibid P.25, Parsons and Propaganda

84. Brian Orr Thereformation.info.com November 11th 2011, Orr provides a detailed description of the capture and execution of Sir John Oldcastle

85. Peter Milward, S.J, *Elizabethan Shakespeare*, Florida, Sapienta press, 2007, P.48 , Milward gives examples of Sir John Oldcastle as a follower of Wycliffe

86. Peter Ackroyd, *Shakespeare the Biography,* P.269 and P.279, Examples of the anger caused by Shakespeare's comical depiction of Sir John Oldcastle

87. John Speed *The theatre of Great Britain* 1611

88. Thomas Fuller "The history of the Worthies of England" 1811 John Nichols

89. Peter Milward, *Elizabethan Shakespeare,* P.48 Milward gives examples of the lampooning of Sir John Oldcastle, John Speeds reaction

90. John Yamamoto-Wilson, http://www.academia.edu/1106934/Shakespeare_Robert_Persons_and_the_Christian_Directory 2016   P.4 Wilson remarks on Peter Milwards observations on the similarities between Hamlets "To be or not to be" speech and Parsons phraseology.

91. Peter Ackroyd, *Shakespeare the biography* P.23 John Shakespeare's testament of faith

92. Stephanie A .Mann, *Supremacy and survival: The English reformation* supremacyandsurvival.blogspot.com/2012/.../catholic-oxford-martyrs.html ,July 5th 2012

93. Peter Ackroyd, *Shakespeare, The Biography* P.415 Robert Catesby

94. John Whitehead, local Oxford historian passed on this information regarding The Catesby family

95. Yeoman William Norton, http://yeomenoftheguard.com/biographies11.htm 13th July 2008, Informative site with biographies of each man involved in the Gunpowder plot, including the Oxford meetings.

96. Bruce Robinson, *The Gunpowder plot*, www.bbc.co.uk/history/british/civil.../gunpowder_robinson_01.shtml   29th March 2011
listing of events surrounding the Gunpowder plot

97. Peter Ackroyd. *Shakespeare the Biography*
P.416 Susannah Shakespeare cited for her failure to receive Holy communion at Easter

98. Former Cambridge scholar William Ritchie informed me of the King James Bibles editing process

99. Charles Nicholl *Shakespeare and his contemporaries*
P.17 National portrait gallery publications 2005, Nicholls mentions Macaulay's fantastic description of King James

100. Stanley Wells, *Is it true what they say about Shakespeare?* Ebrington, Long Barn books
P.109 Wells entertaining book first directed me to this lovely Jonson & Shakespeare imagining by Kipling.

101. Rudyard Kipling, *Proofs of Holy Writ*, Strand magazine, April, 1934

102. Malcolm X, *The Autobiography of Malcolm X*, P.185

103. The Malcolm X visit to the student Union was gratefully brought to my attention by Russia today journalist and author Dan Glazebrook, the human rights activist speech is available to view on Youtube.

104. Mary Edmond, *Rare Sir William*
P.23 Fascinating information connecting Matthew Gwynn with associates of Shakespeare

105. Jonathan Bate, *The Genius of Shakespeare*
P.217, It is from Bates book that I first came across the story of the three prophesying Weird sisters at the gates of St Johns as well as the supposition that Shakespeare heard of this spectacle from John Davenant.

106. Mary Edmond, *Rare sir William* p.23 – 24

107. Dr Emma Smith, *A treasure lost and regained* , November 11th, 2011, Lecture at the Bodleian library
All of the information for this section is heavily indebted to the remarkable research of formidable Shakespeare expert Dr Emma Smith.

108. Susan Stamberg, *Meet Joseph Duveen, The savvy art dealer who sold European masterpieces,* NPR.org March 9th 2015

109. Dr Emma Smith, *A treasure lost and regained,*
All information from XCIX again gleaned from Dr Emma Smiths research.

110. Clutterbuck, L.A & , Dooner W.T, The bond of sacrifice; a biographical record of all British officers who fell in the Great war, London Anglo-African pub, contractors, 1917
P.409.

111. James Shapiro, *Contested Will, Who wrote Shakespeare* , London, Faber and Faber, 2010
P.267, Frances Mere's praise in his Palladis Tamia

112. Katherine Duncan Jones, *Reading Shakespeare's Sonnets, The Arden edition*, London, Bloomsbury publishing, 2010
P.10-P.11 Duncan-Jones gives an insight into an extremely busy period in Shakespeare's life.

113. Brian O'Farrell, *Shakespeare's Patron, William Herbert, Third Earl of Pembroke* 1580-1630, London, Continuum International publishing group, 2011
P.3 Pembroke's men

114. Ibid P.5 Mary Sidney's importance as Patron of poets and the influence of Sir Phillip Sidney.

115. Ibid, P.8, Pembroke's Tutor at New College

116. Ibid P.16 The Mary Fitton scandal

117. Ibid P.18-19 Attacks on Pembroke's character

118. Ibid P.53 March 19th, 1604, Pembroke was the first spokesman at King James first meeting of Parliament

119. Ibid P.49-P.50 The importance of the masques and the first collaboration between Jonson and Jones

120. Ibid P.69 Pembroke given control of the staging of plays

121. Ibid P.77 Pembroke's position as the undisputed patron of poets

122. Ibid P.108

123. Katherine Duncan Jones, *Shakespeare's sonnets,* London, Bloomsbury Arden Shakespeare, 2010
P.384, Duncan Jones notes the offensive suggestion that the addressee of sonnet 135 is promiscuous and that her vagina has been enlarged due to her promiscuity

124. Don Patterson, *Reading Shakespeare's sonnets*, London, Faber and Faber 2010
P.410 Patterson in his fun filled take on the sonnets, remarks on the implication that there is more than one lover called Will involved in sonnet 135, and that this implication pleases the intuition of the Pembrokites

125. Brian O'Farrell *Shakespeare's Patron*
P.91 Dedication to the Herberts.

126. Ibid, P.106-P.107 Pembroke as protector

127. Alfred Armstrong, *Odd books, Reviews and news of very strange books*, https://oddbooks. co.uk/harris/book/fh_manshakespeare.html 2008,
Highly entertaining site reviewing odd books, such as "Shakespeare the man"

128. Brian O'Farrell, *Shakespeare's Patron* P.4

129. Ibid. P.106 Duke of Newcastle's comments

130. Chris Peters, Oxford historian pointed out the humorous notion of King James eternally looking down on Pembroke

131. Paul Collins, *The book of WILLIAM, How Shakespeare's first folio conquered the world*, New York, USA 2009, P.98 Interesting account of Samuel Johnson's efforts to edit Shakespeare's works.

132. Oscar Wilde, *The Portrait of Mr W.H*, London, Hesperus Press, 2003
P.9, The idea that the dedicatee was not born wealthy

133. Oscar Wilde, *The Portrait of Mr W.H*
P.13 The supposition W.H was a young actor

134. Preface allegedly written by a Hadrian Dorrell in the first reprint of Willobie his Avisa

135. Don Foster, Author unknown, *Tales of a literary Detective*, New York, Henry Holt and company, {2000}, P.36, Fascinating shared acquaintances between Shakespeare and Will Peter

136. John Whitehead, Again heavily indebted to Johns generous imparting of local knowledge of the land that once housed the Austins

137. Dave Richardson, *Oxford Pubs*, Stroud, Amberly publishing
P.20-21, The Kings Arms origins.

138. Grace Ippola, *Revising Shakespeare* , Harvard University press
P.81 Mention of G.R Hibbards conclusion.

139. Graham Holderness, *Tales from Shakespeare, creative collisions*
P.65, interesting account of John Reynolds

140. James Shapiro, *Shakespeare the Kings man*, Dazzler Media, BBC,
Episode 1, The great Shakespeare expert James Shapiro paints an entertaining picture of Hampton court packed with two very different factions, the players and the puritans

141. Karen Kay, http://www.britaininprint.net/study_tools/hamlet_sources.html

142. Peter Ackroyd, *Shakespeare the Biography,* P.127

143. Mark Hendricks, *Hamlet, Elsinore and an exploded world May 1st 2011*,
Shakespearebyanothername.blogspot.co.uk
Hendricks interesting article brought my attention to the banquet and though I agree with Hendricks that it was highly unlikely that Shakespeare was at the Christ Church dinner I believe Thomas Kyd probably was, and perhaps inspired by the events that took place at the dinner.

144. Peter Ackroyd, *Shakespeare, the Biography,*
P.122, The school of night

145. Peter Milward S.J, *Elizabethan Shakespeare*
P.104-P.105, Milward coincidentally compares Robert Dudley to Claudius and Sir William Cecil, Lord Burghley to Polonius

146. Mark Hendricks, *Hamlet, Elsinore and an exploded world May 1st 2011,*
Shakespearebyanothername.blogspot.co.uk
Clever observation by Hendricks, Twas caviar to the General... General Laski !

147. Thomas Nashe Preface to Robert Greene's *Menaphon* 1589

148. Albert E Jack *PMLA- Vol 4 to vol 125, no 5* published by Modern language association 1905
Jack provides interesting information regarding Kyd and Ur Hamlet

149. Ian Topham www.mysteriousbritain.co.uk/occult/john-dee.html

150. Peter Ackroyd, *Shakespeare the Biography,*
P.189 The interrogation and death of Thomas Kyd.

151. Nicholas Rowe, *The works of William Shakespeare*, 1709

152. Stanley Wells, *Is it true what they say about Shakespeare?*
P.114 Wells Speculation on the origins of both Rowe and Dennis musings on Shakespeare's
objectives for writing The Merry wives of Windsor

153. John Dennis, *introduction to the Comical Gallant,* 1702

154. J.M Nosworthy *Notes on Henry Porter, Modern language review* P.517-521 Published by
Modern Humanities research association October 1940,
Nosworthy is a noted example of one who has linked Shakespeare's Merry wives to Porter's Angry
women.

155. http://www.beggarsbush.org.uk/henry-porter-the-two-angry-women-of-abington-
1598/#more-511 March 27th 2011, Porters collaborations and praises from Frances Meres

156. Ibid, Porters debts to Henslowe

157. Ibid , The murder of Porter and the last days of his killer, John Day.

158. Elizabeth Sandis, *Oxford and the painted room* pamphlet produced by Oxford preservation
trust-2015

159. Jonathan Bate, *Eric Rassmussen Shakespeare, RSC –William Shakespeare and others,
Collaborative plays*, Hampshire, 2013

160. Don Foster, Author unknown
P.25, Date of Thorpe's publication.

161. Ibid, P.49, "Literary sleuth"-not exactly how a college professor would wish to be identified

162. Ibid, P.4 Fosters talents utilised by probers and prosecutors

163. Ibid P.25 Similarities to Shakespeare's dedication in the Rape of Lucrece

164. Ibid, P.25-P.26 Fosters interesting comparison between lines from Richard II and the Elegy.

165. Ibid, Excellent account of the Exeter city recorder's report. P.31-P.35

166. Ibid, P.35 Drew's escape

167. Ibid P.51, The backlash from Wells, Duncan-Jones,Vickers

168. William .Niederkorn, A scholar recants on his "Shakespeare" Discovery, *New York Times,* June 20th, 2002.

169. Don Foster, Author Unknown
P.36, Links between Shakespeare and William Peter.

170. Richard Abrams, *Meet the Peters, Early modern literary studies 8.2* September 2002, http:purl. oclc/emls/08-2/abrapete.html
Fascinating, detailed study of William Peters family.

171. Ibid P.17

172. Ibid P29

173. John Barton, *Playing Shakespeare*, Television series,
Episode 1, The two traditions, London weekend ITV, 1982, Barton gives a wonderful talk on the naturalistic tendencies of Shakespeare compared to his contemporaries,

174. Ben Jonson's famous remarks on Shakespeare in the preface of the 1623 First folio of Shakespeare's works

175. Paul Collins, *The book of WILLIAM, how Shakespeare's first folio conquered the world,*
P.30 Collins gives examples of the Oxford men's tributes in his excellent book.

176. Dr Emma Smith, *Oxford and the painted room* pamphlet produced by Oxford preservation trust-2015

177. Elizabeth Sandis, *Oxford and the painted room* pamphlet produced by Oxford preservation trust-2015

Select Bibliography

Peter Ackroyd, *Shakespeare the Biography*, London, Random house, {2005} ISBN 9780749386559

John Aubrey, *Brief Lives,* Hampshire, The Folio society limited,{1979}

Jonathan Bate, *The Genius of Shakespeare*, London, Picador, {2008}, ISBN 978-0-330-45843-6

Paul Collins, *The book of William, How Shakespeare's First Folio conquered the world,* New York, Bloomsbury,{2009} ISBN 13:978-1-59691-196-6

Katherine Duncan Jones, *Shakespeare, An Ungentle life*, London ,A & C Publishers ltd,{2010} ISBN 978 1 408 12508 3

Katherine Duncan Jones, *Reading Shakespeare's Sonnets, The Arden edition*, London, Bloomsbury publishing,{2010} ISBN 978-1-4080-1797-5

Mary Edmond, Rare *Sir William Davenant, Poet Laureate-Playwright-Civil war General-Restoration theatre manager*- Manchester, Manchester University Press,{ 1987} ISBN 0-7190-2286-X

Don Foster, *Author unknown, Tales of a literary Detective*, New York, Henry Holt and company, {2000} ISBN 0-8050-6357-9

Germaine Greer, *Shakespeare's wife*, New York, HarperCollins publishers {2007} ISBN 978-0-06-1537

Peter Milward S.J., *Elizabethan Shakespeare*, Florida, Sapientia press, {2007} ISBN 978-1-932589-47-4

Charles Nicholl, *Shakespeare and his contemporaries*, London, National portrait Gallery publications, {2005} ISBN 1 85514 367 4

David Nokes, *Samuel johnson, A life*, London, Faber and Faber, {2009} ISBN 978-0-571-22636-8

Brian O Farrell, *Shakespeare's patron,*
William Herbert, Third Earl of Pembroke 1580-1630, Politics, Patronage and power, London, Continuum international publishing group {2011} ISBN 978-1441-11636-9

Don Patterson, *Reading Shakespeare's Sonnets*, London, Faber and Faber, {2010} ISBN 978-0-571-24505-5

Dave Richardson, *Oxford pubs,* Stroud, Amberly Publishing, ISBN 9781445647289

James Shapiro, *Contested Will, Who wrote Shakespeare* , London, Faber and Faber, (2010) ISBN 978-0-571-23577-3

Stanley Wells, *Is it true what they say about Shakespeare* ?,Gloucestershire, Long barn books,{2008} ISBN 13: 978-1-902421-23-0

Fiction

Henry Porter , *The Two Angry women of Abingdon* Henry {1598}

Oscar Wilde, *The Portrait of Mr W.H*, London, Hesperus Press, {2003} ISBN 1-84391-031-4

Henry Willobie, Willobie His Avisa , HardPress Publishing, ISBN 9781313108706

Select Documentaries

In Search of Shakespeare, Director David Wallace, BBC {2004} U.K

William Shakespeare The Bard of Avon, Cromwell productions {1995}

Shakespeare the Kings man, Directed by Steven Clarke, Green Bay for BBC, {1996} UK

Select Lectures

Dr Emma Smith*, A treasure lost and regained* , November 11th {2011}, Bodleian library

Stanley Wells, *The genius of Shakespeare*, September 3rd {2015} Blackwell Hall, Weston library

Acknowledgements

I am extremely grateful to Joe Wilkins and his sublime formatting skills, the proof reading and editing skills of Anna Soprano, Adam Dale and Dan Glazebrook, and indebted to the vast local knowledge of Simon Image, Catherine Wolfe Smith, Chris Peters and John Whitehead, and eternally thankful for the support of Susannah Cartwright, Alistair Cornell and Neil Walker
The contributions from the following artists have been invaluable, Danny Connor, Tanya Denise, Barbara Gorayska, Jon Patterson and Alex Singleton.

List of Illustrations and photographs

Sweete Wittie Shakespeare by Susannah Cartwright
Approximate site of William Knells death {Tom McDonnell}
William Davenant's baptism by Tanya Dempsey
Davenant road {Tom McDonnell}
Shakespeare and The inn keepers wife, Alex singleton
William Davenant by Jon Patterson
Gunpowder plotters at the Catherine Wheel inn, Oxford by Danny Connor
Great minds, Shakespeare and the king discuss the bible at the Bodleian by Alex Singleton
The weird sisters at St Johns by Alex Singleton
Momento Mori, Hamlet at the Kings arms by Barbara Gorayska

Lightning Source UK Ltd.
Milton Keynes UK
UKOW06f0210110416

271999UK00003B/5/P